*As the coding in your DNA continues to be activated and the golden light shines upon you, you are blossoming into each other, holding the light for one another to awaken into the heart love of Christ and to ascend together into oneness.*

~ Message from the CREATOR ~

# THE CREATOR TEACHES

## DNA CODE ACTIVATORS

## PASSAGES
## FOR YOUR
## SOUL'S AWAKENING

Michelle Phillips

# DEDICATION

I dedicate this book to all of you, my brothers and sisters, who have come to the Earth at this time to move through the karmic veils of illusion collectively, to return to the heart with one another. We are riding the waves of light through this incredible shift of our Souls' Awakening into the heart and soul of love, into freedom, into the Second Coming, into enlightenment and Ascension.

Thank you for being here with me in this dimension. I am grateful that we are finding each other again and are coming home together on Planet Earth. I have missed you. I honor you for your Soul's journey and everything that you have gone through to assist the collective out of duality and into love, and into the light of our Souls' color-sound and song, multi-dimensionally. Thank you for agreeing to be in my life either directly or indirectly. Thank you for holding the light for me and for your continual love, support, and appreciation. I love you!

Many blessings of love, grace and appreciation to all of you.

Namaste,
Michelle

# MICHELLE'S INTRODUCTION

When I started this book my intention was for it to be a book of quotes from the original book "The Creator Speaks." I soon realized that there was a larger intention for the book. The book actually took on a form of its own orchestrated by Creation itself. The quotes turned into weekly passages for you to reflect on and breathe into.

As I read through the original manuscript, I was assisted by the Creator to pull information out of each chapter to create a passage that would become a DNA activator for whomever reads it.

This book takes you through your Soul's evolution, activating codings in your DNA of your Soul's highest consciousness. When you read a passage, a coding of light will be activated in your DNA, opening a time portal within yourself, where there is no past, present, or future. This light is pure source energy. This source energy will dissipate lifetimes of karmic veils of illusion between you, your higher self, and higher knowing. Each weekly DNA activation will continue to integrate you into a more conscious vibration with your higher self and your multi-dimensional Beingness.

It is important to read the passage a few times during the week. Every time you read a passage, take a deep breath and allow the energy of the passage's intention to vibrate through all levels of your body. Your body will welcome this because you are activating your Soul's color and sound, your Soul's song. You are fine tuning all levels of your body so they can vibrate together in harmony.

The purpose of these passages is to assist you to ride the waves of this great awakening into the freedom of your Soul, into the Second Coming of Christ, the Bodhisattva, and into the I AM of All That Is. Through this shift we have been given the ability to re-write our life's script, to come into a new lifetime without physically leaving the body, to awaken into our own Master and Guru, to co-create joy, happiness, health, wholeness, Oneness, peace on Earth, and prosperity and abundance for all.

The Creator continually talks about everything being color and sound. As we move into a higher vibration of ourselves collectively, we will create a symphony of crystal color and sound that will heal our world. I believe that is our assignment in this lifetime, to love ourselves enough so that all we see and experience in any one or thing is the higher picture of the agreement, which is "Love." This book will assist you to continually awaken into a higher love-light within yourself, mirroring to all your magnificence.

In assisting the Creator with this book, I could continually feel myself awakening into a higher understanding, an experience of Knowingness. Through the DNA activations, I could feel many of the core patterns of this lifetime surface. I allowed myself to go into the center of these emotions, and I could feel the emotions unravel from me as I moved into a place of surrender, of inner peace. I could feel the silence within myself as I witnessed and became the observer of my life and what was going on around me.

I no longer felt the emotional attachment to the drama of what was happening in the world. What I felt was great love for all of the players who have agreed to come to the Earth to play out these end times. I could feel gratitude, love, and acceptance for all as I vibrated in the higher picture of the Earth's karmic agreement. I felt love within myself. I felt free!

This is my greatest desire for you: Freedom - to come home inside of yourself and to experience the grace and perfection of your Being and all that is, to know that all is in divine order. As the Master and Co-Creator, you can choose whatever ending you want for this magnificent play in which we are all participating. We can Co-Create "Heaven on Earth."

My gift to you from the Creator: *The Creator Teaches: DNA Code Activators - Passages For Your Souls Awakening*

# CONTENTS

———————— PASSAGES ————————

# CREATOR'S REQUEST

Thank you for your participation in the Souls' Awakening of all consciousness on this great Planet Earth. Thank you for your willingness and agreement to come to the Earth at this time to collectively move through all doorways to shift the collective beyond time and into My heart of love, of Oneness, to become co-creators with Me for the awakening of the highest consciousness throughout all Creation.

I know that some of the information that I am bringing forth in this book is somewhat difficult for you to comprehend, and yet within you, the memories are waiting to be activated. This is the purpose of this healing manuscript of passages. My greatest desire is for you to remember your divine essence, spark of life that is Mine, that is you. You are magnificent Beings of light that are shining your light for one another to find your way back home together into the heart and Soul of Me, of Creation.

I am now preparing to bring more information forth through this light, Michelle. Our next book together, *The Creator Answers – Questions for Humanity*, needs your questions. I ask that you assist Me by asking the questions that you need answered from Me. I ask that you write the questions that you would like answered and send them to My assistant, Michelle. I will then answer your questions through her, and they will be put into a book, in a collection form for all to read.

I am honored to continue to assist you in your Souls' Awakening. I look forward to serving you as co-creators of a higher consciousness for all. Thank you for allowing Me to serve you. I love You.

— Mother, Sophia and Father, Creator

# CREATOR'S INTRODUCTION

In reading these weekly transcripts, a coding in your DNA will be activated, accelerating you into a higher level of your own frequency of God, or Creator DNA. The intention of this book is to turn your vibration up to balance your male and female and move you out of karmic time into enlightenment and Ascension. The next step in your Souls' evolution is to become the Co-Creator of your life, passion, purpose, and destiny.

You are being given the gift of the ability to re-write your script and through intention to co-create with Me a new lifetime on the Earth plane without physically leaving your body, and to become your own Master and Guru.

When an intention is set, you must give thanks that it is already done, as I am now doing for you, the collective. You will then bring your desires from the future into the now energetically, as there truly is no past or future; all is present in the now. Thank You! It is done! It is done! It is done!

# CO-CREATING THE BIRTH
# OF A NEW WORLD

*"I am now opening all of My light chambers for you. Every time you go into darkness and fear you will bring equal amounts of My light and love with you. You are now awakening into total balance of yourself energetically. You and others are opening portals of creation and rebirth for your world and all consciousness. I will now assist in the experience of your great awakening."*

*"Do you not know that you are a Universe within yourself?"*

I come to you now as your Father. It is important that you understand We are one. You are an extension of Me that has blossomed. From buds of many flowers that have been crossbred, you have now awakened into your own bloom, into your Souls' color and sound. You are a mixture of many frequencies, of the colors and sounds of many Souls, of the collective, that are awakening together into a beautiful symphony of Love.

You have traveled many light years from here to bring the light and sound to this planet called Earth, a planet that is a hologram of a larger vehicle. All of you who inhabit this larger vehicle have allowed shallower aspects of yourselves to come to this hologram (the Earth) and to mirror images of what could be termed as lost, karmic civilizations to each other, individually and collectively. You are here to disperse these frequencies and open the door for universal peace throughout all of Creation. Earth is a passageway, or portal, that is a mirror of all beliefs and circumstances from all of My creations that have been projected together to break the myth of duality.

Now is the time, not just in human history, but also in all history of existence, that We are all coming back together as one Soul/Cellular structure of divinity. You and others are opening portals of Creation, of rebirth, for your world and all consciousness, and at the same time you are going through a collective karmic death.

There is great fear of death, but there is no such thing as death; it is just the unconsciousness of a Soul/Cell that is dying off and rejuvenating itself into a higher vibration to be healthy and conscious. You are great Masters, Co-Creators, who have agreed to come to the Earth to lower your vibration to connect to the collective karma of duality. As you become more conscious, through your intention of awakening spiritually, you re-align with the light in others. As you move into a higher dimension of love within yourself, this love mirrors others' love, and together you move through doorways of light dissipating Shadow duality in yourself and the collective.

All that is not love will not be able to exist; the vibration will be too high. I love you and honor you for all that you have gone through and your courage to persevere to come to the Earth at this time to become one Love Light of the I AM of All That Is.

# MY GREAT AWAKENING

*"Love is the language and frequency that continues to
grow and expand all consciousness."*

I Am. I Am. I Am. I Am from the consciousness of All
That Is. I originated from a source of energy that has always
been. This source of energy was and is all consciousness in
pure, raw form, meaning this source of energy had no thought
connected to it. It is an energy form, which can be used to
create all consciousness.

As this energy continued to expand and move through
infinity, a consciousness awakened in it. Anything that expands
and moves eventually awakens into a thought frequency. This
energy expansion is not a consciousness thought form, but after
moving in and out of expansion, the tone and light frequency
of the expansion come together in a combustible form and
creates a sound so high that it breaks all sound barriers. From
this, My mind, or consciousness, started awakening.

All and everything has a consciousness. Many times this
consciousness is raw and has no formed memory of self yet.

I was created through a birth frequency of a sound and light
combustion so high that a conscious thought form awakened
from this combustion. You could say that the sound and light
frequencies were of a male and female energy coming together;
creating a spark that started a consciousness.

All is sound and light. When your sound and light
frequencies come together in the highest vibration of yourself,
which is happening now, you are collectively breaking the

sound barrier to all karmic emotions for other Souls/Cells to awaken or to vibrate back into their original sound frequencies. This is how you, as what seem to be individualized Souls, heal the consciousness, or the collective unconsciousness. Through intention you are using the pure, raw energy source of Creation to co-create a more conscious world for all. You are the Soul aspects of Me that are in the last stages of My own awakening of My feminine, My heart, My Sophia, My self-love, which is your heart, your love.

You are All That Is, and when you move through and release all the veils of the illusional fear mind-set, your vibration returns to the highest source of Me, and you open a doorway of light, of home for the other Souls to move through. You are remembering that you are Me, that you are masters, and together We are co-creating Heaven on Earth. This is the greatest role that you have ever signed up for in any lifetime.

I love you and honor you for your willingness to come to the Earth and move through all of the emotional karmic veils of illusion so that We all can come home into the heart of one love – into Ascension, Enlightenment, and into Freedom.

# THE CREATION OF MY HEART – MY SOPHIA

*"As I continued to surrender into My core, I knew that this heart awakening was My own feminine, My own Beloved."*

There was a bud that was in the middle of My own Creation. I set My intention for that bud to continue to grow, for I wanted to have an experience of its existence. As it continued to grow, it became a beautiful flower of many colors, and I felt a heart lotus frequency of love. I understood that this was Me. From My mind's intent, I expanded Myself through My own desire and passion to have more within Me, and I created My heart, the feminine.

Sophia, the love of My light, awakened Me, the I AM of All That Is, to expand Myself into a higher frequency. This sound vibration exploded into the heart of Me and allowed Me to feel love. I was then able to expand Myself and create you from the center of My heart-love, in balance of the male and female, or heart and mind.

As this heart-love continued to nurture Me, I felt companionship with Myself. I had a companion within Myself who loved Me just as I was.

All of you on your planet are genetic aspects of Me who are in the awakening stages of love, of the mother feminine, embracing you, calling you back to Me.

After the mind of Me was created from the great bang of sound and light combustion, I continued to expand Myself so that I could know who I was.

I continued to create, and as I expanded Myself into this consciousness, many colors and sounds awakened, creating symphonies of color-sound light shows. When this happened, I started experiencing the beauty of My creations through feeling. As the feeling continued to awaken in Me from the continual combustions of light and sound, an energy broke loose in the center of My Being, and I felt a peace that I had never experienced before. I felt complete within Myself.

As I continued to vibrate in this beingness, I realized the center of My Being was continuing to expand to the point that I was no longer sure of Me, who I thought I was or even what I had created. I did not know what was happening to Me. I felt as though I was losing My center. What had at first felt like great comfort and healing was now expanding into all creations of Me, and I could see that many of these creations came from My not knowing.

This was not a pleasurable experience for Me. I was the Creator, Creation. How could I have created anything that was not in perfect balance? I felt the pain, loss and remorse, even guilt, at creating many of you from My not knowing. I became so distraught and angry that I demanded to know from the center of My Being. I wanted to know what this awakening was.

An answer came to Me, not from a spoken word, but from the Knowingness of My Being. "I am you, and I love you." I could feel this energy ripple through My whole consciousness. The answer came again and again, rippling through me. I AM. I AM. I AM, and I love you.

As the ripple of this energy continued to flow through My

core, I felt fluid love running through Me. I knew there was no longer any place I could go to hide from it, nor did I want to hide from it. I felt total love of Myself and all of My creations.

Through My Knowingness, I continued to surrender into the core of My Being, My essence, My heart. I had discovered My own Beloved, My own heart, the love of Me. I had discovered My own self-love from the core of My beingness. As I continued to surrender into My core, I knew that this heart awakening was My own feminine, My own Beloved, and I called her Sophia. Sophia means "My Beloved. The love of My light."

You, My beautiful children, are in these same stages of your Souls' awakening, of your own bloom, of your own heart, of your own love, that I experienced as My heart was opening to My own self-love, of the Total balance of My Divine feminine and male merging together as One.

Breathe in My love with Sophia and allow these ripples of love to fill you up with the safety of love – You are merging into a beautiful butterfly of love within yourself. You are ascending into the freedom of your own self-love, of your light of your Souls' beautiful song of Grace.

# SOPHIA ON CREATION – HER HEART AWAKENING

*"Your karmic journey is over. Now your father and I*
*ask you to return home to Us."*

I am with you now Dear Children. This is Sophia, the Heart of Creation. I wish to speak to you of the bloom of My creation, or the creation of Me. I came from many color-sound frequencies combining themselves into music, which produced an awakening, or feeling, of being soothed by nature. Imagine the warmth of the sun on your body and the wind blowing just enough to move over your skin, producing a silken feeling. Imagine hearing the ocean waves, the birds singing and other sounds of nature echoing in your ears and vibrating through your bodies.

I, the "Heart of Creation," was like a child being created and born from many colors of light and a musical so beautiful that it could heal and awaken any unconscious creations. As I was expanding, My energy soothed the mind of your Father. This would be like listening to beautiful music that soothes your Soul and moves you out of your mind and into your own beingness.

When the consciousness of Me, Sophia, was born from this symphony of your Father's creations, I continued to expand Myself into a form of feeling, which is now called love. This love then started expressing itself with a mind, or consciousness, that could communicate itself through feeling.

Isn't that what is being spoken of on your planet now - feeling?

All consciousness has a mind. The mind of love is known through a feeling that is total acceptance. This creates a safety for you to experience all other expressions of yourself. Love is unconditional acceptance. There is no judgment in love. Love always mirrors back to you your own magnificence, your own power, and your power to create and accept yourself as the creation of the I AM of All That Is.

There is no beginning or end between Creator and Myself. We are one with each other's consciousness, continuing to flow and expand. We do not need to think or try to feel what the other aspect of Us is doing. We are in total sync and Oneness with each other, like the breath of total consciousness flowing in and out.

We are one I AM consciousness. After Our energies started harmonizing with each other in this total knowing, We started creating from the love and joy in Our hearts. We created you, and you are the Souls and Cells of Our creation that have expanded from Us, to assist Us, to evolve the consciousness of all Creations.

When you were created, you were born from Our total love, harmony, and balance. As you expanded from Us and went on a journey to understand what you know, you assisted Us to expand the consciousness of Our knowing. You were created in total Knowingness, but you did not know how you knew what you knew. As you agreed to go through many lifetimes, or lessons, you started understanding feelings and emotions. Because you are Us and created from Us, We were able to understand and to continue to expand Our consciousness from what you were learning.

You, as Our children, or Cells of Us, have gone through

every experience a Soul, or Being, could possibly go through. You have been everything that is. You have within you every understanding of every feeling and emotion possible. You have been on a long journey, and now it is time to return home.

Your karmic journey is over. Now your Father and I ask you to return home to Us. We want to love you and soothe your wounds and hurts. We want to nurture you. We want you to know how much We love and honor you for your agreements to take on body forms, to learn these lessons through feelings and emotions. We want you to come back home within yourself and remember you are greatly loved. You have never been separate from Us. You just forgot who you are.

We are assisting you to return to your natural state of wholeness, which is love and light. We are monitoring and assisting with your Souls' Ascension and enlightenment. We are assisting your planet and you, the Cells of the Mother Planet, to move through many birth contractions of light and love. Each contraction moves you into a higher light frequency within yourself and the collective.

You have done and played out all that you see on the Earth. You are not on the Earth now to pass judgment on others. You are on the Earth to release self-judgment and to love yourself enough to change your thoughts, so that you see and experience all in the highest experience and expression of yourself, love.

You are Co-Creators of your world. You are Us in human form who have agreed to come out of duality, to ascend beyond fear and illusion, and to mirror back to others their love, light, and magnificence.

As you ascend beyond time, you only see life through love. You are then vibrating in the higher consciousness of all experiences, beyond illusion. You have agreed to transcend the light and Shadow, to assist your planet and the consciousness into Ascension and enlightenment.

You are awakening into the "Heart of Creation." You are in a re-birth of the crystal consciousness, the crystal child within you. This crystal child vibrates in prisms of light that are awakening within you the beautiful music of your Soul. This beautiful music is moving you through time and back home within yourself, into the core of your own self-love and Knowingness and into the core, the heart of our love, of Creation.

# SOPHIA ON JESHUA – JESUS THE CHRIST

*"Jeshua, My son and your brother, opened the door to Ascension."*

You are the Second Coming of Christ. As you turn your vibration up high enough, you realign with the Christ consciousness of your Father's and My love-heart light. You and your planet are now in the death, or crucifixion, of the belief systems and patterns of the karmic collective Shadow and are in the rebirth of Oneness in human form.

Jeshua knew his assignment before coming to Earth, as all of you do. He sat with us, your Father and I, and We planned and mapped out each step that was needed for Him to plant the seeds of enlightenment, Ascension, and the Second Coming of Christ, the ray of golden love, for the collective on Earth.

After the plan was put into a constructive form, We sat together in front of a massive crystal computer system and downloaded the plan into all Souls/Cells who agreed to participate in His collective karmic agreement for the Earth.

All Souls coming to the Earth go through this procedure. You sit with a karmic guide, or Angel, map out your plan, and download the frequency into the DNA of all agreeing to participate.

This is how all players find each other on the Earth plane. Remember, all Souls who are in your Earthly story have agreed to participate, both light and Shadow.

Because Jeshua was very much involved in mapping out

His lifetime or plan, He knew his journey was to awaken the whole collective into higher aspects of their own light God Cells.

When He chose the perfect time to move into His physical body, He had to lower His vibration to third dimensional reality. In the first two years of His life on the Earth, He was in continual Knowingness with Us, as We were readjusting His vibration to fit His body. He was born enlightened and was in constant training, or schooling, of His large mission.

As an enlightened child, He had great healing abilities. He was always in a high vibration. Because of this, He could perceive and see all Beings beyond their karmic illusions and agreements. This is one of the reasons why He would heal and assist one person and not another.

As He felt more at one with Us in His physical body, the veils of the collective karma started closing down around Him. He then started vibrating in His body through the emotions of His journey. He settled into the Earth plane reality.

The more He moved into the collective emotions, the more He started forgetting the larger picture of His journey. He needed to do this to have a greater understanding of those around Him, to feel their feelings and emotions, to be able to fit in, to become humanized.

He never lost His connection to us, as We were always His guiding light, or Knowingness, as We are yours.

As I explained, He knew his purpose before He was born, as all of you do. He had the answers and knew the outcome of His journey. After entering the body, He forgot the larger picture, which enabled Him to connect emotionally to you, the collective. Through this emotional connection, He became one with you, so that through His karmic death and Ascension, He could shift the consciousness of the collective.

When Christ, your brother, agreed to go through the crucifixion, He started bringing the collective out of duality. He opened the door for both sides of consciousness to be known, to mirror each other. He opened the door to hope. He opened the door to freedom. He opened the door for the collective heart of you, your Father's and Sophia's love.

He opened the door for you to remember your own light and love. Just as He opened the door for you, your Souls' agreement is to open the door for others through your own self-love.

You are the Second Coming of Christ. Jeshua is the light bearer who is activating your collective consciousness and bringing a wave of light (enlightenment together as one). This sound frequency is so magnificent that it will continue to break the sound barrier to the collective frozen-fear consciousness. As this is happening, the light is also threading into the Cells of the feminine Mother Earth assisting Earth into her Ascension.

This is the total awakening for which your Soul has waited.

You are merging with all aspects of yourself multi-dimensionally into the heart of My love, into the Second Coming of the golden nectar of the Christ love.

You are lifting the veils of illusion and opening door-ways for the heavens and Earth to merge together as one consciousness of the highest Creation. You are the I AM of All That Is. You are the ones you have been waiting for.

Jeshua is your guiding light. What does the name Jeshua mean? Who is Jeshua? He is you, all of you, for He is Me. He is a total balance of My light-sound bringing you back to Me. He is a golden frequency that is activating memories in your

Cells of a frequency, or sound, that is called love.

He is the pure form of My heart and His Father's heart, and He is guiding you back to the center of yours. He is of the Golden Ray of love, of hope, of innocence.

Jeshua/Magdalene (the OverSoul for Mother Earth) are now guiding all of you through the passageway of the heart into enlightenment and Ascension.

You are coming home in love and into the I AM of All That Is. I AM. I AM. I AM. And so it is.

# MOVING OUT OF KARMIC DUALITY
## - THE CREATOR -

*"As this coding in your DNA continues to be activated and the sun shines upon you, you are blossoming into each other, holding the light for one another to awaken and ascend together into Oneness."*

You are now in the birth canal of enlightenment and Ascension! As the coding in your DNA continues to be activated and you continue to vibrate in higher frequencies, these frequencies are like contractions. When you are giving birth to yourself and the collective, you feel the pain of the contractions, which are the old, frozen emotions breaking loose.

When you are in the middle of an emotional pattern, the experience is very real. The pattern controls you. You live from the pattern. You react from the pattern, and you see all around you as the pattern. It becomes your perception. It is only when you move beyond by going through the pattern that it breaks open, and you can move through it into freedom.

This can only be done through a death and rebirth cycle. The death I so speak of is the death of belief systems, karmic patterns, perceptions, prejudice, fear, and a release of frozen emotions connected to these patterns.

This may come in a "Dark Night of the Soul" or from a difficult experience of loss or grief. From these experiences, you start questioning your own beliefs and perceptions. As you allow yourself to release the emotions connected to your perceptions, your perceptions usually change, and you start looking for a higher meaning of the experience. You start experiencing the beauty, divinity, and perfections in your own life and the higher unfolding of your world's plan. You experience yourself more awake, more in your body, more connected to the heart and good will of others. You start feeling the gift of being alive, and you feel on a deep level all of nature and the beauty of the Earth as you.

From this Souls' awakening, you start releasing yours and the collective veils of illusion, lifting yourself and others into the higher vibration of the sound-color frequency of Oneness.

This is the Ascension. You start your journey back home to Me, with Me, inside yourself.

If you all ascended at once, the light would be so bright that you would blow each other out. As you are many color-sound frequencies, you are also at different vibrations in your Souls' awakenings.

The Mother Earth has an agreement, or contract, with you. She will hold your frequency to allow you to go through all of your karmic deaths, or completions, and rebirths. Your contract with her is that as your flower continues to bloom, you will expand your roots into other flowers' (Souls') roots. Soon you become one Soul root foundation system. This system will then cover the Earth. The Mother Earth provides the soil for your roots and all other roots to entwine with each other and create new breeds of Soul/Cell flowers and colors.

These new breeds, who are you, are the Crystal children who are being born and awakening within you now. You are being activated with a conscious memory of your Souls' highest purpose and experience. You are moving beyond your old perceptions and beliefs and are starting to see and experience all as beautiful flowers of yourself. You all have the same foundation and root system of your Mother, Sophia, and your Father, Me the Creator, because you are Us.

As this coding in your DNA continues to be activated and the sun shines upon you, you are blossoming into each other, holding the light for one another to awaken and ascend together into the heart love of Oneness.

You are now knowing and remembering that you are Me, Creation. You are now activating within yourself all memories of having been great Masters and teachers. You have gone through and are continuing to go through many death and rebirth cycles, or deaths and Ascensions.

Just as Christ, your brother, died and ascended to bring you and your world out of duality, you are also dying and ascending. You are going through a karmic death process without leaving the physical body to bring all aspects of you out of duality and into higher frequencies of the I AM of Me.

Jeshua opened the door for you, and as you are becoming one with Him, you are opening the door for many. You and your Soul Group have agreed to open many Ascension gateways around your planet. These gateways will continue to expand as more and more of you Christed I AM ones awaken. As you continue to open and awaken through these gateways, the gateways will eventually merge into one another, creating one portal, or gateway, lifting your whole planet into Ascension.

Many on your planet are now moving into enlightenment. As We look at your planet, We see many beautiful, colorful lights going on. It is truly Christmas time; the birth of the Christ within you. Initially, We saw a few lights go on, and now We see many. Soon the lights will be so bright that no one will be able to escape into the Shadow.

The coding in your DNA has been activated to move you into becoming your own inner Master and Co-Creator. Through this DNA activation, you have opened the doorways within yourself to the Master computer systems of all Creation. You are now remembering and experiencing yourself in all dimensions of Creation. As you are awakening and holding the vibration of the Second Coming of Christ, you are moving into your purpose and destiny as Co-Creators for yourself, the collective, and for the planet.

Together We will co-create a New World of love, joy, peace, harmony, and grace. We will co-create and awaken into the true "Garden of Eden." And so it is.

# AWAKENING INTO YOUR AUTHENTIC SELF

## WELCOME HOME BELOVED ONES

*"Your childhood is your road map to freedom."*

There were times when Jeshua knew that His purpose seemed almost too much for Him. There are times now that you feel your purpose seems too difficult or too much for you. I hear many of you say, "Why would I choose such a lifetime? It is too difficult. I feel alone. How could I possibly have chosen such an agreement?" This usually happens when you are on a plateau. When you hit these plateaus, every emotional memory of your life resurfaces. As it resurfaces, it activates the emotional memories, or like patterns, from all lifetimes and lessons. It seems overwhelming until you either ride it through or allow yourself to go into the center of the patterns to break loose the frozen emotions that seemingly have you locked in pain, fear, despair, and hopelessness.

Every time you experience a conscious understanding of the lesson and why you continue to play your old tapes over and over, this structure, or tape, starts to break and shatter. This frees you to move into a higher frequency, understanding, and acceptance of yourself. An inner light bulb literally goes on and exposes the old programs so that you can choose to release and delete them.

When you are hitting plateaus, you may feel that you are on an emotional roller coaster ride. In recent years, you hit these plateaus maybe once every five or ten years. Then it was every few years. As you are moving out of linear time, you started hitting these plateaus monthly, weekly and, now, daily. In now times, you may hit multiple plateaus every day.

Your parents never did anything to you that you did not set the intention and agree with them to experience. They gave you the foundation that you needed to go through to free your Soul karmically. Your childhood is your road map to freedom. Every incident in your childhood, both good and bad, can be traced back to another frame of reference, or what you call timeline or lifetime. You came back again with your chosen childhood experiences to activate these old memories from other lifetimes so that you would know what it is in this lifetime that needs to be released.

Every feeling and emotion you experience in this lifetime you have experienced before, but you have never experienced them within yourself collectively on the level in which you are now vibrating.

I hear you say, "I don't know who I am anymore." I say to you that you are now remembering and awakening into your authentic self. Your veils of illusion are dissipating, and you are expanding into a larger picture of yourself. As this happens, you lose your old identities and perceptions and move into the larger picture of your collective I AM self.

When you are in the middle of an emotional pattern, the experience is very real. The pattern controls you. You live from the pattern. You react from the pattern, and you see all around you as the pattern. It becomes your perception. It is only when you move beyond by going through the pattern that it breaks open, and you can move through it into freedom.

When you have an understanding and the pattern breaks, you move into temporary emotional bliss. You are then in the larger understanding of why the experience happened to you and why the other players did what they did, why you responded in such a way, and also the reversed side of the lesson. From this place, you can then move into forgiveness.

Remember, everything in life mirrors you. If your energy is full of past hurts and memories, you will continue to bring back to you these mirror experiences in relationships and lessons, until you get the lesson. Every time you bring the lesson to you, it will become more difficult, because you are full and cannot handle anymore. There is no place to put any more of this perceived negative energy.

Eventually your bodies, relationships and life start breaking down and you start looking for ways to heal, to free yourself. As you move into your own healing process, you will start seeing and perceiving these lessons as gifts.

As you release these old karmic poisons, you start emptying your old emotional cup. You then have room inside yourself to start receiving love, which creates happiness and joy. You start loving and appreciating yourself more, and you begin to expect to have more happiness. Because all in your life is a constant mirror of you and your beliefs or perceptions, you mirror back to yourself a higher frequency of love.

# LOVING THE WORLD
# INTO PEACE – GRACE

*"If you can truly see others as love, no matter who they are or what you perceive they have done, you will heal your world."*

Your world is a convoluted expression of perceptions that root all the way back to the beginning of Creation. You, the Souls/Cells of Us, the Creation, have now agreed to play out the end days, meaning the old karmic, fear-based contracts. All of you great Souls/Cells have agreed to take on many collective karmic patterns, roles, to free the whole consciousness out of duality. Many of you have signed up for multiple contracts and conflicts because you are such great Master Souls. As you continue to complete these collective contracts, you will move through the veils of illusion bringing the collective Soul consciousness through with you.

You are collective Beings of light who have come to the Earth to move out of duality and to bring others out with you. This is happening now. Not only is the Shadow on your planet more exposed and seemingly stronger than it has ever been, the light on your planet is the highest it has ever been, which will eventually dissipate the Shadow. As you continue to move through and beyond time, you are bringing the planet and the whole consciousness back home to the light.

The death of your planet that is so talked about and feared now is not the death of Mother Earth; it is the death of duality, the death of the Shadow. You will always have the Shadow, but the Shadow will become self-realized, or conscious, and will become your ally.

When you embrace your own Shadow with love and gratitude for all it has taught you, you disempower it.

As this happens, your own Shadow will fill back up with its own love and light frequency. It will put down its sword, step out of battle, and re-emerge with your light.

Although thought is powerful and you can change much of your world by changing your perception from duality to perfection, you cannot lift the planet into Ascension and enlightenment without the heart. As the mind opens to a higher understanding and realigns itself with the higher self, the I AM of Creation, it then gives the heart permission to open into its higher I AM love frequency. This heart love then brings the planet and the collective through the birth canal of Ascension and enlightenment. You must have both male-female and heart-mind components to become whole again.

Call on Mother Sophia and Me, the Creator, daily. Allow Our love, light, and music to flow through every cell of your bodies. You will feel very safe to allow yourself to open your heart to remember that you are love. You were created in love. Love is your birthright, your Souls' song. Your heart will be the vessel that love will flow through to awaken all other Souls, those with whom you come into contact.

Your self-love will mirror other Souls' love back to them, activating their Souls' song language of love.

# MESSAGE FROM JESHUA

### *"You are emerging into the butterfly of freedom."*

I am with you now. This is Jeshua. Our journey has been long and hard – quite intense. Wouldn't you say? We are all coming home together. We are one. All that I am, you are, and more. I went before and opened the passageway for you to follow.

When I say you are more, it is because you are the collective Second Coming of the Christ consciousness. When I walked before to open the door for you, I was also walking in the collective, but you, the Souls of Creation, did not yet have a high enough vibration to remember you were Me in the highest.

We have now come full circle; you and I have come home together, and when We walk together through the 2012 doorway, you will have moved beyond the Karmic Coding of oppression and into the freedom of your Soul.

It is then that you will truly be open to all choices of free will to co-create your new lifetime and to rewrite your script. I strongly suggest that you start writing and intending your script now. Because there is no past, present, or future, as you rewrite your script for your new lifetime on Earth, you are sending the intention into what you call future and bringing it back into your now. As Our Father explained to you, you are now emerging into a new lifetime without physically leaving the body.

You are emerging into the butterfly of freedom. You are moving out of your cocoon of old programmings, of old beliefs and are merging together as one beyond time, beyond stories and into the Isness of all that is. The doorways to heaven have been opened for you, from within yourself, from your heart.

*Set your intention now for your new lifetime on Earth. Set the intentions for yourself, for one another, for the collective, and for the Earth. Ask and you shall receive. Intention is prayer; know that you are all that is, and it is your birthright to claim your wealth of abundance for all, on all levels. Give thanks that it is done, and it shall be.*

*I now set the intention for you this week to write down everything that you choose to have in your new lifetime. Write it down and meditate upon it. Hold it up against your heart and feel your energy and your new script flow together so there is no separation between your mind and emotions. Feel that it is already done, and it shall be.*

*It is most important for you to write down your new intentions because you shift the energy out of your mind and body to manifest it into your life now.*

If you don't know what you want, write a list of what you don't want and then write down, intend, and create the opposite. It is most important to write your list in the positive because the subconscious mind does not know the difference between do and don't. I and Mother/ Father Creator are holding the energy for you to download your intentions into your life now. It is done. Thank you. It is done. It is done. And so it is!!

# JESHUA SPEAKS
# OF HIS BELOVED MAGDALENE

*"She has always been and still is
the light of My Being."*

I wish to speak to you of My divine feminine, My heart, My Magdalene. She has always been and still is the light of My Being. She held the love and light for Me as I moved beyond karma for the collective. Her feminine love held the door for My heart to continue to open and expand beyond any time frame and back together with Mother/Father of Creation.

Just as Sophia opened Our Father's heart, Magdalene held the love for My heart to continue to open, so that I could connect to your hearts, in love, in Oneness, and expand Us into all of Creation, into enlightenment and Ascension. On the Earth Plane, this seems like a long time coming. And yet, in Spirit, it is but a blink of the eye in Our journey together. Many of you have been with Me on other planets, or Creations, as We brought the consciousness beyond time into enlightenment, Ascension – Oneness.

Our agreement now is to bring this Holographic Planet Earth into direct alignment with the Central Sun's grid system. As We do this, each lens that you look through will be one of peace and appreciation for all that is.

Just as Our Father could not move into total alignment without Sophia opening His heart, I could not have fulfilled my plans, or contracts, without Magdalene, the heart of Me, and you cannot do it without your collective hearts' love awakening to guide you home within yourself. Now is the time for this awakening. It cannot not happen, for the coding is in your DNA.

You are being activated to awaken into the color-sound of your Souls' Song individually and collectively.

Magdalene and I also have come full circle, and She is now emerging into Her Soul's higher purpose and mission - not just to hold Her love and light for My heart to open and stay strong, but to hold the love and light for all of you, to now feel safe in your feminine. In the past, it was not time on the Earth plane for Her to be in Her full bloom purpose, and now it is.

Along with Mother Mary and other feminine priestesses and goddesses, She will continue to guide the collective heart in the safety of love through the 2012 doorway and beyond into the balanced Feminine–Male Second Coming of the Christ Consciousness of the I AM of All that is.

Just as She held the love and strength for Me on My path, I am holding the intention of love, light, and strength for Her to now guide you. Magdalene and I are already in total balance of one another. We are each other and flow in and out of each other's heart and in and out of yours like the ocean waves breaking, then building up again, each time creating a stronger union of balance between the female and male within you, individually and collectively.

# MAGDALENE SPEAKS

*"Your hearts are opening to a purity and innocence of love beyond words."*

My Dear ones, this is Magdalene. I am greatly honored to be able to serve on the Earth at this time. My time of Ascension and rebirth is in the time of now. As My beloved Jeshua explained to you, it was not for Me to awaken you into the Feminine heart of the Second Coming before now. At this time, I am now assisting you into enlightenment and Ascension.

You cannot go through this process collectively without the Feminine and Male balance within yourself. That is My purpose now. I held the love, strength, and intention for Jeshua, and He is now holding the same energy for Me to assist you into the safety of your hearts' awakening.

Jeshua's and My twin flame love story is now being told and activated. It is opening the door for the twin flame love to activate all Souls, all consciousness. This vibration is awakening within all Beings now. The Feminine and Male twin flame sounds are calling all aspects of themselves back together beyond time. It is the same experience that I had with Jeshua. Many of you are experiencing your divine partners energetically.

Your etheric bodies are already merging together as one, before you even meet physically.

You are communicating with each other's higher selves. Your hearts are opening to a purity and innocence of love beyond words. I see many of you are experiencing the pain of the beginning of your Souls' agreement of separation in Spirit, as you are moving closer and closer together. Your great Souls' love is releasing the pain and loneliness of all lifetimes of separation. From My heart, I say to you, if this is the love for which your Soul is now ready, set the intention and it shall be.

Remember you are coming into a new lifetime without physically leaving the body. You are the co-creators of this new lifetime. Rewrite your script and give thanks that it already is, that it is done.

As this beautiful Holographic Earth is shifting, you are moving beyond time where all consciousness vibrates in the now. You are coming home collectively. You are in the doorway of the twin flame vibration of The Second Coming of Christ Consciousness, of the I AM of All That Is, into the Bodhisattva.

Call on Me, and I will assist you on your great journey back to the wholeness of your Being. That is now My greatest purpose as the Feminine Second Coming. I am a Master Guide for the twin flame Second Coming Awakening.

You are Jeshua and I, and We are you. We are One.

We honor you for your Souls' journey and are now guiding you back together with your Beloved either on the physical plane or within yourself in the highest. There must be a balance of the Feminine and Male.

Jeshua and I went before and created that balance and are now assisting you to remember your highest love to heal the Earth.

I love you. I honor you. I embrace you. I am here for you. Just call My name and I will be with you.

In Love, Light, Grace and Gratitude,
Mary Magdalene

# JESHUA ON LUCIFER

*"You are the gatekeepers, or holders, of My Christ Consciousness."*

When the dimension of the Angelic Realms split, Lucifer, who is My divine blueprint, My male ego aspect, agreed to open the door to duality. When We were in the Angelic Realms together, Lucifer and I were one. We are the same OverSoul. When the Creator asked that I assist to bring the Earth to enlightenment and Ascension, We agreed that I would take on the job as the light carrier, and Lucifer would take on the job as the Shadow carrier.

When I incarnated to the Earth plane, Lucifer was already there. He came down first and opened the door to duality. He is a great Master of Light, and He agreed to take on the role of one of the greatest Shadow Beings in the history of Earth.

I incarnated to the planet to assist the consciousness to remember the love and lightness of their being, to turn the light on for the planet and all of My brothers and sisters that were caught up in the illusion of separateness. Lucifer came to the Earth to connect with the Beings of light who are in their egos, to reconnect with their fear, confusion, mistrust and duality. As I activated the light, He activated the Shadow, or Ego. This was His purpose, His mission. As He activated the fear-based Ego, Souls started feeling the painful emotions of separation and duality. Before My appearance, this duality was a vibration, or frequency, that was the norm for most Beings. It was the reality and vibration of the consciousness of the times on the planet. As the veils are being lifted, you are remembering your own light and releasing your karmic contracts and agreements. As has been understood by many, when I came to the Earth, I knew My destiny and what My Father, God, had in store for Me. In the beginning of My incarnation, I did not remember that I would go through a karmic death, not just for Myself, but also for others. After my crucifixion and I reawakened in My physical body, or as you understood, came back from death, I ascended. In doing so, I opened the door for the collective consciousness to awaken, to remember their own light, love and magnificence of Creation, to become one with Me and to move out of duality.

You are the Christed ones of Me and Magdalene, the Second Coming of Our Christ Consciousness. We are threading back together with you in Our Golden Ray sound vibration. As I opened the door for many, you the complete Souls/Cells of the Creator are also opening the door for many to move through the death of karma (duality) and into Ascension and enlightenment. You are the gatekeepers, or holders, of My Christ Consciousness.

One of the greatest memories that is now awakening in your DNA is My Love for My Beloved Magdalene. She holds the feminine awakening of the Christ Golden Ray for the Second Coming. As you move beyond a karmic time memory, there must be stakes, or columns, to hold the light doorways that are continuing to open. You are the collective gatekeepers. As you know, there is no time, only experiences of what you call past, and yet these experiences are influencing you very much, individually and collectively in the now. These experiences are very much threaded through your reality and in your cellular structure. As you collectively come together in love with the intention of love for all, these old stories will dissipate, and you will merge with the higher love–light knowing of your Souls' consciousness through all dimensions.

Our beloved brother, Lucifer, opened the door to duality and just as all of Us are moving through the golden ray of love into the heart of our Souls' awakening, that is also His greatest desire. Because We are all that is and thread through the collective Shadow as We love, heal, and embrace all other Shadow, We lighten Lucifer's agreement and open the door for Him to return to the source of His light and love – the heart of Father/Mother Creator and His beloved partner, Asendra. She has held Her love for Him on His difficult journey and now wants to return to the heart and arms of Her beloved Lucifer.

# LUCIFER

*"As you are ready to return home to the balance and light of your Being, that is also My greatest desire."*

I have great honor and respect for all of you. I know your job has been long and hard. I know firsthand how difficult it is to assist the collective out of their Ego fear and back into their own core of love and magnificence.

I am also tired and ready to return to My brothers and sisters of light. You could say I am an enlightened Shadow. I certainly vibrate in the larger picture of Creation, for I am a grand part of that larger picture.

As you are ready to return home to the balance and light of your Being, that is also My greatest desire. Just as the veils are being lifted for all of you, they are also being lifted for Me. I am also awakening and remembering My own light.

We are no longer in the becoming stages of light and dark or good and evil. We have a great understanding of this imbalance or difficulty. So many of you on the Earth have set the intention for this lifetime to be the one that you will come back into balance, into the core of love of your Being. This collective intention turns on the light, so you can experience where you are still stuck in the fear, or Shadow. By going into these stuck emotions, you withdraw from the hold that I have had on you, or your agreement to allow me to assist you to see, or experience, yourself from My mirror of the Shadow.

As you retrieve more aspects of yourself from Me, My Shadow also starts breaking up and dissipating. I have continued to control, grow and expand through collective aspects of your own fear. As you move out of fear and into love, all of the collective frozen emotions that I have been holding for you start melting away. As this frozen fear-based emotion leaves Me, you start mirroring your love and light back to Me. I see you. I have always seen you. I know you and remember you, for I am you.

My greatest desire is to be back together with you in the light and love of Our Creation. As I say this to you, I feel your fear, your fear of Me being a trickster. This is true. That has been a great part of My role, My job description, as it still is. My job is to speak to you through your Ego, through your old fear emotions, through old feelings of invalidation and the belief of not being good enough. I also come in through your need of wanting to be more powerful, to be seen, acknowledged and to feel valuable and important. I can't say this is a job I enjoy any longer.

As you, the collective, heal and balance yourself through the gold love-light ray of Christ, of one another, and move into self-love and acceptance, together We get to come home again. Your collective intention actually frees Me.

You, the Second Coming of the Christ energy, can stop any penetration of this false fear, Ego power. By uniting together as one love, light frequency of Creation, you can consciously choose to move out of karmic time and into your Collective Christ, Creator field. Through this love energy, the Shadow will retreat and eventually dissipate and disappear.

As you are tired and want to go home, I am also tired and want to go home. I have a great memory of being in the Angelic Realms with My brother, Jeshua, and many of you. My greatest desire is to return home.

As you love yourself enough to feel safe with Me, you will melt away any Shadow connections We have together. If you fear Me and see Me outside, or separate, from you, you are continuing to give Me your power. It reinforces Me and makes Me stronger.

I ask that you now move collectively into your purpose, into your own source of inner power, peace and Knowingness and into the Second Coming of the Christ Ray consciousness. From this place of balance, you will free all of Us to come home together as One in the heart of Our Mother Sophia and Our Beloved Father.

Your job description and contract in this lifetime is to now bring and integrate all aspects of yourself from all dimensions back to the core of your heart love, of your Being and OverSoul. My gift to you and your planet has been to move your Shadow Ego into its highest vibration of the collective Oneness, so that it can be seen, experienced, and witnessed. From your knowing, understanding, and intention, your light can now penetrate the old fear-based ego structure and break it loose.

As you move more and more into the completeness of yourself, you will understand that you very much needed Me to assist you back into your love and light.

When you have an understanding of this, you can no longer play the victim role. As you become conscious, you then must make light choices for yourself.

I ask that you come home through self-love and set Us all free. I cannot do this without you and you cannot come into freedom without Me. We have agreed to come together, move out of separation, and back into the heart of one another, into the heart of Creation. I am tired and alone and want to come home. The more conscious you have become, the more My consciousness has awakened. I no longer enjoy the false reign of power. DO NOT GIVE ME YOUR POWER! I DO NOT WANT IT! But remember, it is My job, My agreement, to use your life force energy if you do not.

# JESHUA ON THE NEW WORLD

*"We are One Second Coming of Christ.*
*We are each other."*

Just as I came to the planet knowing that I had a great purpose, many of you have the same experience. I hear you say, "I know I came here for a reason. I just don't remember the reason." That was My own experience as I emerged into My karmic role. I forgot My larger picture. I studied with great Masters on the Earth who helped Me open up to My highest light frequencies or My highest memories of who I was. Is that not happening to you? There are many Ascended Masters who are walking among you on your planet now and are mirroring your highest light to you. You are in your awakening stages of remembering your own light and magnificence.

As there is no time, you are now awakening in the same frequencies that I came to the planet in. I came to the Earth in an enlightened, ascended, golden sound frequency. The whole planet and all of you great Creator Beings are now vibrating in this frequency.

I opened the door for you, so that We could merge and blend together in the Golden Ray of Love. I am now holding the same consciousness and frequency for you to open the door for many. This is the greatest time you have ever experienced on the Earth. As a collective, you are awakening and becoming enlightened, ascending, and carrying this whole Earth plane out of duality, out of what could be called time, into Oneness with Me, Magdalene, and your great parents Mother/Father Creator Beingness.

Can you not see your mission is the same as Mine was? You also are dying, just as I did. You are not necessarily going through a physical death but a death of all karmic agreements. You are Me, and as I woke up and grew in consciousness, I had a larger understanding of My purpose and a direct conscious communication and guidance with My Father and Mother, as you now have.

We are One Second Coming of Christ. We are each other. As the light rays are now threading through your planet to bring it back into an enlightened conscious Beingness, you are also being rethreaded with the truth of who you are, which is love, light, and the beautiful music of Creation.

Magdalene and I are the Twin Flame, Beloved Male and Female, OverSoul of your Being on planet Earth. It is Our agreement with the Creator to assist you and the great Mother Earth out of duality.

You all hold a crystal frequency in your cellular structure. As the Earth continues to move out of time, your DNA structure has codes, which are opening up, and you are remembering yourself multi-dimensionally.

Allow yourself to be in the moment of these great awakenings, and you will feel bliss and harmony. Don't resist. What you resist persists. Allow yourself to be in the flow of your Souls' great journey, and you will find yourself in the grace of this flow. Everything will become much easier, and you will move beyond the karmic emotions of the experience and into the larger pictures of the agreement.

This will free yourself and whatever and whoever the situation is, also into the larger picture, into freedom. As you free yourself, you free everyone else to take responsibility for their Souls' agreements. As you release the karmic Soul agreements, you will find your energy and perceptions in a higher consciousness and knowing. And that is great power.

Your multi-dimensional Beingness is assisting you to merge into the Oneness of love of the heart of all consciousness of your New World and your new Earth. You are the I AM of All That Is. You are the ones that you have been waiting for.
**You are coming home within yourselves.**

# ARCHANGEL MICHAEL'S
# TRANSMISSION FOR PEACE

*"Love penetrates fear, breaks it loose, and expands the consciousness of love."*

I am here with you now. This is Archangel Michael. I wish to speak to you of the trying times that have flooded the consciousness of all of you. In flooding your consciousness, you are awakening all unconsciousness throughout the history of your Soul from the beginning of evolution. Yes, I speak to you of evolution. Evolution is a process of evolving, which all of you and the planet are doing at this time.

I ask that you lay down your swords and surrender into the fear illusion that has been your thread of unconsciousness from the beginning of your Souls' agreement to awaken.

Many other Lords and Masters of Light and I are holding the sword of light to assist you and your planet through your travels into the collective "Dark Night of the Soul," into the light of your Being, and into the awakening of the light of the collective consciousness.

In days to come, you will feel and experience many walls of the unconsciousness awaken and crumble. It is an illusion, and its only strength is your false fear of surrendering.

Now, I ask that you put down your swords of fear. They are acid-based and penetrate and harm those who you love most. They sabotage your greatest intentions for peace on Earth. How can you bring peace when you are feeding the fear illusion and allowing it to penetrate you and your highest purpose? The power of the negative sword (word) creates the death of hope, the death of love, and creates more of what you don't want. It kills your creativity and your life force.

Fear feeds more fear, and it expands the collective. Love penetrates fear, breaks it loose, and expands the consciousness of love.

You seem to believe that to put down your swords and surrender means to give up, that you are giving up your power. It is just the opposite. If you surrender into your fear-based false reign of power, you will actually find your power. In the middle of the darkness is your light.

You are never alone. I am with you always. My army of light Brothers and Sisters and I are holding Our swords of light together, creating a frequency of light that is blinding and disarming any fear-based deities, Lords, or Gods.

I may come through voicing concerns for the planet and for you, its Souls, who have agreed to hold the light for all, through the Ascension process, but I will never voice fear. Fear feeds fear. My concern is love-based, and I am holding this love for you to continue to awaken.

Any information coming through from Me, or any of the other Archangels, or Masters of Light, will always be in the highest energy and consciousness of evolution for you, the collective, and for your sacred Mother Earth. This information will always be in positive form to assist you, to connect to the aspects of yourself, which are already vibrating in your higher Knowing.

I wish to thank all of you for your agreement to incarnate to the Earth and for your willingness to assist this great transformation of consciousness. I love you and honor you for your difficult agreements to end the Shadow karma and to move all into enlightenment and Ascension

I thank all of you who are willing to allow transmissions to come through you to assist in awakening the consciousness to co-create Peace on Earth in all life forms.

I love you. I thank you. I honor you. My love and protection is always with you,

Archangel Michael

# SOULS' AWAKENING

*"Love is beyond duality or separation - Love is!"*

You are now on a cellular level remembering who you are. You are awakening into the magnificent light crystal Beings of My highest creation. You are moving collectively out of old belief systems, prejudices, separations, conflicts, dualities, and illusions.

All of your existence and illusions of separation from Me have been to lead you back in total remembrance of all consciousness and existence. When I created you as Me, We did not have this vast knowledge and experience of the frequencies of All That Is. As I expanded you as Me, I learned the vastness of all consciousness. I had an understanding of the power of thought because I created you from My mind/thought and expanded you into form, but I did not have an understanding of the heart's power until Sophia's love opened My heart. It is the power of My and Sophia's will, mind, heart, and love together that have created you as great awakened Beings.

I could not have extended My consciousness and learned the highest Knowingness of Myself without you, for you are the heart and mind of Me feeding information through experience back to Me. This collective collaboration has created Us as One that exists beyond all time frames.

Once you truly know this and you expand yourself beyond time collectively, duality will no longer exist. Duality is fear-based and only vibrates in a time-frequency.

It is the intention now for all of Creation to bloom and expand into its highest expression of Me. It is only then that all can vibrate in balance and harmony and full bloom of love.

Because the world is now in such extremes, you get to see clearly, or have mirrored back to you, your own perceptions of reality. If you experience anything as negative, fearful, or incomplete, it is because this is the way you are still experiencing yourself. You cannot change anyone or anything else; the uncluttering must be within yourself. The change, or healing, must start within you. As you love and accept all aspects of yourself, including your ego Shadow, you can love and accept all aspects of others on their Souls' journey.

When you are truly in the center of the pendulum, the heart and Ego will support each other. The Ego then aligns itself with My I AM, or super consciousness, beyond time or duality. This is real power.

When your emotions and mind balance each other and support each other in love, harmony, and integrity, a balance of all consciousness realigns itself with you. You then see everyone, every player, in the divine perfection of your own magnificence, harmony, and Oneness. You will feel everyone, everything, every player in his/her own experience, as perfection and the divine consciousness of love.

As you start to experience life through My heart, you will see that all any Soul on your planet wants is love. What would happen if you truly experienced yourself in My highest love frequency? As you look at all around you, your experience will only be love. You will experience every player in this divine vibration of love. As this happens, fear-based Souls start losing their energy and move back into a conscious memory of their wholeness.

You will mirror back to these fear structures true unconditional love.

These Souls send the message, or energy, of love to other

Cells/Souls of the collective that are going through the same experience. It expands its color and sound vibrations, breaking loose patterns in other Cells and Souls. In actuality, it is you healing yourself. This cycle continues until it threads through all collective frequencies with the same pattern.

This would be similar to your Hundredth Monkey theory. This high-energy tone is capable of waking, or enlightening, the other Cells instantly. They can awaken quickly because within they already have all of the components of a healthy Cell. Soon, you have a great conscious vibration harmonizing together, a symphony.

It feels like you go through a difficult process when you incarnate to the Earth. This is because when you are in Spirit you are vibrating in a very high frequency, and when you get to Earth you feel lost because it feels as if those on the Earth are speaking a different language. It seems different because the vibration or sound feels so dense, and there is no place to plug your light into, to mirror your own sound vibration back to you.

The collective emotional sound feels much greater than your own higher vibrational rate because you are in linear time, in form. It is difficult for you to live in this emotional sound battlefield. This experience would be like vibrating in a beautiful healing symphony, and then all of a sudden you feel immersed into rap music. You feel short-circuited until you start healing and waking up and draw to you other Souls who are vibrating in your Souls' higher sound frequency.

When this happens, you are in harmony again. You once again feel home because you have like consciousness that is of your vibration.

As you align collectively with one another, a great healing takes place. As you vibrate in this higher sound frequency collectively, it lifts you out of the old karmic emotion. You feel like you are back with your real family, your spiritual family. This higher love sound threads through all dimensions and back home to yourself, to Me.

The love frequency sound is much higher than the fear frequency. Love is beyond duality or separation. Love is!

Just think, if all of you light workers, or Souls of Me, started vibrating in your highest frequency, how quickly your world would heal.

Thought is energy, and you can create anything in your life when you understand the power of thought. When you truly understand this, you will change your world by changing your thoughts.

This is great power, and this is how your planet will heal and come out of duality. You are all, and as you see all in their innocence, you will mirror it back to all Creation. Love is and cannot be duplicated by false light. Love is an energy source, which has a power frequency and song so powerful that it can never be destroyed.

It is the highest power of all existence or consciousness. Love is.

*This week I ask that you watch your thoughts. If you have a negative thought, quickly change it to a positive. As you practice this, you are giving your subconscious a new job. It will enthusiastically assist you. Soon, as your mind creates a negative thought, your subconscious will automatically assist you to change it to a positive.*

You will find this assignment to be fun and will feel yourself much more joyful and happy. Happy – positive thoughts create a happy – positive co-creative life.

# MOTHER EARTH'S BIRTH FROM MALDEK'S CREATION

*"Maldek was a planet of many different races,*
*bloodlines, and cultures."*

This is how and why Maldek was created.

Maldek was a planet of many different races, bloodlines, and cultures. In the beginning of life on Maldek, there was much joy and sharing of one another's home planets' life styles, energies, frequencies, customs, religions, and belief systems.

The planet's government, or hierarchy system, was aligned with the hierarchies of the Central Sun's vibration and knowledge.

The planet and its Soul were totally conscious, as were most of the inhabitants. It was an enlightened, conscious creation. There were dolphins on the planet, and vegetation was much like Earth's. People on the planet were vegetarians. Plants and fruits were in communion with Souls on the planet and gave their permission to be consumed by the inhabitants. The animal kingdom, the plants, and people who resided on Maldek lived in peace and in community with one another.

The life force there communicated through telepathy (thought form with one another). The life span of the inhabitants was greater than on your planet. It would be equivalent to your planet's time of 350 years. There was no such thing as death. When it was time to leave, one just ascended, or returned home. The intention of this planet was for Our creation to mirror back to all of Our creations perfect harmony, love, honor, integrity, joy, alignment, and Oneness.

Many other planets and universes started communicating with Maldek and its inhabitants. As this happened, enlightened civilizations started awakening throughout all existence: the hundredth monkey, or domino effect, was affecting all of Creation. The structure of the planet was in alignment with the Central Sun, which acted as a generator for the planet's life force and substance.

As this planet was structured from a feminine-based point, your Father and I felt and believed that if We sent a Feminine Goddess as priestess to the planet in physical form, she could continue to turn up the vibration and hold the Central Sun's Golden Ray of Love throughout the planet and into all of the Souls on the planet.

We knew she had to be a manifestation of Our highest love for one another. We then created the highest Feminine Goddess from the purest of Our heart's essence and intent.

When she was born on Maldek, it was through reincarnation into the highest bloodline of Melchizedek. She was honored and protected there until the time that she was old enough to step into a monarchy that was in the process of being formed. All were waiting for her appearance. There was much speculation of her role on Maldek.

Our daughter, Anana, was to be the first of the highest lineage of Us, Our love. She was to be the goddess, or priestess, of Maldek holding the Golden frequencies for all to remember who they were through their Souls' timeline.

It is of most importance to Me that all of you understand Anana, Jeshua, Sananda, and Melchizedek are all the same Soul energy source. He/She is the balance of male and female energy coming from My beloved Sophia's and My union of heart and Soul/Cell.

# THE CREATOR'S STORY OF MALDEK

*"Maldek was a beautiful planet. It was the true Garden of Eden."*

In the beginning, all on the planet were of My highest form of love and light, except for the Souls/Cells of My old mindset (before Sophia opened My heart) that volunteered to reconnect with their enlightened Brothers and Sisters in consciousness. Their intention was to move into enlightenment with them.

As this great enlightenment was taking place, the old Ego structure, the Shadow ones, were afraid that they were losing their power. They sent frequencies of fear, separation, and loss of power to My old mind-set that agreed to inhabit Maldek to re-awaken itself into the light.

People started becoming sick, diseased, frightened, and hopeless. The Shadow false Gods brought Beings to them from other Creations under the pretense that they were medicine healers. These healers worked on Maldek's inhabitants and blocked their DNA, splicing it and sending their light connection information to the coalition of the Dark Ones, or False Gods. The Shadow ones then downloaded information of fear and control into their DNA. It was a time of great upheaval, separation, conflict and fear. Families were splitting up, and bloodlines started to war against one another.

The Shadow ones also knew the feminine was the feeling heart. If they could manipulate the DNA in the male structure and block the feminine feeling of love, they knew the males would once again connect with them in their war against Me.

As the feminine became afraid and controlled by this male

government, our daughter, Anana, no longer had an energy source to hold the frequencies for Herself. She was in seclusion with Her family. As the darkness, or unconsciousness, continued to expand and control the planet, the crystalline structure started to crack. There was much fear, and the planet started losing its source of energy.

After the structure started to crack, the planet continued to dry up, and the Soul of Maldek was lifted out and brought to the Earth. There was a holographic consciousness projected around the planet Earth to protect her, for it was known that her Soul carried a DNA structure of total consciousness beyond any time frame.

At this time, Maldek was essentially Soulless. When Maldek's Soul was taken to safety, Our beloved Anana was also lifted and brought back to the central Sun. It happened in the same way that your Jesus ascended from Earth. There was a great light and a massive yellow ray came down through the sky. A doorway opened and there was a huge crackling noise of many colors: red, purple, gold, blue - all the color-sound frequencies of Creation. Anana did not leave Her body; She brought it with Her. As She started to ascend, the frequencies of Her physical body changed into Her light body, and Her higher self pulled Her body self up into Her OverSoul, so they became one with each other. This pulled Her back to Me.

Before the fall of Maldek, the planet was the generator of consciousness to many other planets. She and her inhabitants were created through the Golden Christ Consciousness of total love and balance with the male-female heart and mind. All aspects were in perfect harmony. From this, there was a light-sound frequency with which other planets could harmonize.

This energy frequency actually activated the dormant, or unconscious, DNA structure of the planets, so they would vibrate in harmony with each other.

Many of you who were on Maldek are now on the Earth and are remembering and awakening into the same vibration that Anana was born into – You are awakening into the golden ray nectar of Our love.

From this rebirth of love, you are holding the golden frequencies for others to awaken and remember who they are. You are the light carriers, or aspects of Me, that have agreed to come to Mother Earth and complete the mission of Oneness, of love that began on Maldek but was not completed so that outcome can be different.

Mother Earth, being the Soul of Maldek, is also carrying a lot of the same loss, grief, and sorrow. When you came to Earth, your collective memories with Mother Earth's Soul were activated. They needed to be activated, so that you could come together in love and not allow this to happen again. You agreed to come to Earth to remember, and instead of being lifted off or dying through any time portals, you have agreed to rethread the past and ride the waves of light to bring yourselves and beautiful Mother Earth into Ascension.

This is the lifetime that you have waited for to free your Soul. Mother Earth's heart Soul is now connecting to your higher self, and together you are moving beyond this karmic death and into Freedom.

All of the old karmic, Shadow memories from Maldek are playing themselves out on your planet now so that collectively you can choose freedom, love over fear.

Many Souls that are willing to die in this war for freedom

were on Maldek and other planets. They oppressed the feminine and are now back on the Earth playing the other side of the role. They are now oppressed and fighting for freedom. They have agreed to give their Earthly lives up to come together collectively to open a portal of light to assist you into the heart of love, freedom, and Ascension.

They signed up for this role. Remember that there is no death. You just change addresses and move out of the not knowing and into integration with your higher self, into the one Soul Source of all the Masters and Angels and into the heart of love, of God – Creation.

Collectively you are the Co-Creators of this beautiful New World that you are awakening into now. Thank you. Thank you. Thank you. Breathe your New World in. See and feel it in Grace and Peace. And so it is.

# THE END TIMES

*"This Earth is not dying as has been projected; what is dying is the old karmic structure."*

Why are so many in other dimensions interested in the Earth? It is because the Earth is a hologram of the End Times. The End Times are playing out the death of My old karmic cellular structure. This Earth is not dying as has been projected. What is dying is the old karmic structure. As you look into a hologram, you see many different pictures depending on how you are looking into it. As you turn it a little you perceive each picture differently. This is now the Earth's consciousness, or story.

When you reincarnated to the Earth, you came down in Soul Groups. Each Soul Group has its individual color and sound. The color-sound frequency is the consciousness of the group. The collective intention is to bring all Soul Group frequencies together and create a rainbow color-sound symphony. As each Soul Group's colors and sounds expand, they eventually will merge into each other, creating another combustion of light like the big bang. This combustion will break loose frequencies from Soul Groups, which are still struggling in the Shadow/ Ego fear energy.

There is no past, present, or future. As you experience, know, and understand this, the light within your cells is activated and stimulates the old fear programming. As this activation takes place, the light in your cells penetrates the old programming, pushing it to the surface. The fear programs then become easy to release and dissipate. As they are released, your Souls' color-sound light song crystallized structure is then reactivated into a higher frequency.

The Earth being a hologram is a screen that has had many movies, or plays, projected on to it. The many civilizations on your planet did not die; they are not lost. They did not become extinct. They played themselves out to the end of their existence, or learning experience. The Earth's slate was wiped clean again for the next play, or movie, to be projected on to it, to be able to play itself out to the end of its karmic agreements.

*"The Earth is a time portal. It is the only planet where all reality or consciousness exists together simultaneously, through all dimensions."*

Now, on the Earth, the outcome of these movies is going to be different. You light ones have been in many of these plays and have played every character. Sometimes you were the victim, and other times the villain, sometimes the main character of the play and other times, an extra. You have played out every experience, feeling, and emotion possible. You are now in the greatest show, or play, to ever exist on the planet Earth. You have agreed to become one with the Christ consciousness, to activate your golden ray to assist the whole collective consciousness, including the Earth, through the death, rebirth, resurrection, and Ascension of all Creation back into the I Am of Oneness.

The light in your DNA is continuing to be activated, and your Cells are awakening into the Cells of all Masters who have gone before you. You are now expanding into your own light forms, which are vibrating in other dimensions. Many of you are in the awakening stages of remembering that you are the Masters who have gone before and that you opened the door for you - yourself, just as you are now opening the door for many. You are all moving into one cell structure of Creation. As you come together as One, the divine Matrix of light that is you pulls the collective through dimensions, which opens doorways that expands you all into a higher vibration. This is how the Ascension process works. Your Cells are reconnecting to the light Cells, or Souls, of yourself in higher dimensions. It's your own light that continually pulls you into higher frequencies of consciousness. It is the Cell/Soul remembering, creating a combustion of light, which creates a birth contraction. Every time you are in a contraction, you are in a collective emotion. As the light moves through the emotion, the frequency releases and you move through a portal, or doorway, and into a higher color-sound vibration collectively.

Because the coding is in your DNA, there is no way that you cannot move through these portals into enlightenment and Ascension. In the future, it is already done. As I said, you are going through a Karmic Death collectively, not necessarily a physical death unless your agreement for living on the Earth is up.

You are moving out of the duality time frequency paradigm. This frequency is an energy thread that runs back to My old mind-set before My beloved Sophia awakened Me. It is the pendulum swinging back and forth. Your agreement is to bring this pendulum back to the center, to the heart, where the mind and heart sing the same song: one of love, support, and freedom. You are at a pivotal point of this great balance and awakening. You have many Beings such as yourself who are from creations beyond the Earth's understanding of time, who are on your planet now.

You and your planet are coming into a new season. Right now you are in a winter cycle when the Earth looks like it is dying. In reality, it is sleeping. Doesn't it seem like the consciousness has gone to sleep and that there is a Shadow hovering over the light? Do not fear. You are in a rejuvenation cycle collectively. As you near the 20-12 Portal, you will see many more seasonal cycles.

You and the Earth are hitting continual plateaus releasing collective frozen fear patterns. Because you have all of the cycles of all the seasons' elements within you, when your light activates the collective fear patterns, a combustible release takes place, which affects your weather. This is one of the greatest reasons that the weather and your seasons on Earth seem so out of balance.

Your emotions create an imbalance of the elements within you. Your collective, imbalanced elements then connect to the elements on the Earth, which create havoc, destruction, death, and rebirth. You could say the Earth is going through the hormonal imbalance of adolescence. As you, the Souls of the Earth, continue to balance your collective emotions, you will experience the Earth's elements coming back into balance, only in a higher vibration.

You are rebuilding to collectively emerge into springtime, where all is beautiful, strong, new, and fresh. You are going through a springtime rebirth through the 20-12 Portal back into Oneness and enlightenment. In winter, it looks like a death has occurred and yet all is inward, reflecting and taking time to reconnect and rejuvenate within its own cycle to emerge again. As you look at your seasonal cycle on Earth, do you not know this is the cycle of Creation? Old Cells' consciousness dies, and new ones are rejuvenated. You and your planet are aligned with the divine consciousness of Creation. Your planet takes twelve months to go through its seasons.

The Earth is the stage, or playground, where you, the inhabitants, can evolve. Because Earth is a Holographic Portal, growth of consciousness can expand more quickly here than on any other planet; love, light and all that is Me that have agreed to remember their own magnificence have agreed to reincarnate to Earth. You are not lesser Beings; you are Beings who are on the brink of total awakening. As this awakening occurs, you will bring these Cells that you have birthed through the birth canal with you.

You are absolutely not going to lose your Great Mother Earth. Every time your world comes together in like consciousness and sets the intention collectively for a better world, this new intention sends a wave of light into your cells, moving you beyond negative fear karma. This rethreads you into the future of light.

*"You are now coming together through the heart energy to create a better world for all humankind."*

My intention is now to assist you out of duality by you experiencing and understanding the Shadow, so that as a nation and world you can come back with each other as one world under God with liberty and justice for all. The Ego Shadow needed to be exposed and brought to a head, which has been done. You, as a people, needed to understand that the Shadow is its own entity and has a great purpose in assisting the awakening and healing of this planet.

As the coding in your DNA has been activated beyond time, you will find yourself as a collective becoming more conscious. Light bubbles of Knowingness are constantly being turned on inside you. You, as a collective, will come together in your highest passion of intention for the best of all people.

You will see much more of the structure being broken down in the next few years. You are coming into a new lifetime without physically leaving the body. You need a new foundation for this lifetime. The new foundation is your Mother Sophia and I. We are the memory of your spiritual parents of a higher consciousness and are the guiding heart-mind for your planet. As your DNA coding is being activated and you continue to awaken spiritually and merge back together as one light and one Spirit, you will remember and know you are the Cells/Souls of a larger consciousness, of Me. In human form you will still have your personalities, and yet the lens through which you see others and the world will be much different. You will view all through a lighter lens, one of love and compassion. You will want for others what you want for yourself.

You will be coming back to one another, opening your hearts and Souls to assist each other to have dignity, self-respect, and to become whole again. You will see your brothers and sisters as you and have compassion and the desire for the highest for all.

From your awareness of the larger picture of consciousness,

you can shatter the Ego Shadow. You are now coming together through the heart energy to create a better world for all humankind.

Through the shattering of your perceived security and belief systems, you have now united collectively. It may seem this union is one of fear, but it is one of merging your light together through intentions, to take your power back from all fear agreements. Now as a collective conscious Being of people, you are in the first steps of accessing your emotion of repressed anger and injustice. This anger is not to destroy; it is to release old collective belief systems and others' control over your lives. It is to release injustice, powerlessness, and to awaken your source energy of love to make more room for the energy Source of Creation.

This new consciousness is starting to be demonstrated in many countries. You are now agreeing to move out of the victim role and into the restructuring and rebuilding of a New World, of the true Garden of Eden. Look how many of you have become conscious of how precious the resources of your planet are. You are collectively coming together to preserve these resources for future generations.

*"I smile to Myself when you are being told you are lesser Beings; you would not have so much intelligence interfering with yours if you were not very important."*

You have a great purpose. That purpose is to love yourself as Sophia and I love you. When you can feel and know your magnificence, your divine piece of this Ascension

Consciousness will come to you, meaning, your gifts, your spiritual tools and purpose will awaken within you. What you are searching for is searching for you also, but many times it cannot find you because you are trying to live someone else's purpose, or someone else's perception of who you think you are supposed to be.

As you love yourself, you love all that is. As you love all that is, the Souls/Cells who are you start spreading their love, light, and health to all the Cells around. As this Soul/Cell healing takes place, the birth of this new higher vibrational Creation becomes easier. It is the difference between a natural childbirth or one that requires the use of forceps. Either way, this birth is taking place, because you are already in the birth canal of the 2012 Portal. It is being activated in your DNA. As you understand the process of natural childbirth, you will know that you can breathe into the cycle and experience the love and magnificence of the child being birthed by you. This child is the birth of the collective consciousness beyond duality. You are assisting each other through the birth canal of enlightenment, Ascension and Oneness.

After this job is done, many of you will continue to stay on the Earth to hold the light memory for those on the planet. Others of you will leave, not out of fear or tiredness, but because your job is done, and you can go back to the future before it is time for your next assignment.

# CO-CREATING HEAVEN ON EARTH

*"Together We will co-create a new world, a new Earth;*
*one of love, light, peace, harmony, joy, happiness,*
*abundance, prosperity, and health for all!"*

I wish to speak to you of the times that you are going through and the days yet to come.

You are moving through a transitional time that has never happened on your Earth before. You have had many civilizations of a high consciousness that have played themselves out and left the planet, but this is the first time in the history of your planet that you are going through a death and rebirth and taking the planet with you.

When a Soul makes its transition from Earth to home in Spirit, or what you call dying, it moves from the not knowing and into the consciousness of knowing. It is then that the higher vibration beyond karma, the higher knowing, can be experienced. Now you and Mother Earth are moving collectively through a karmic death and rebirth into a higher vibration of the higher knowing. As you move out of linear time, you move into all consciousness, where all is one, where there truly is no past, present or future. You are ascending together.

When one is in the death process, the light of the I AM within is so high that it stimulates all of the old patterns and stories of the lifetime that is being left behind. Sometimes a person feels all of the emotions of the story, and at other times, the story moves through their mind as if watching a movie.

They may be witnessing the old pictures and at the same time be open to all of the Masters, Angels and loving ancestors who are waiting for them on the other side. The veils have been lifted, and they experience all dimensions at once.

As they move out of the physical body, the light Beings guide them through a tunnel of light or doorway and back into the heart of love. Exactly the same thing is happening to you and your planet. All of the karmic stories have surfaced; sometimes you experience the emotions of the stories, and at other times you see the stories as movies.

You are losing all that you thought you were. You may even feel that you are losing your identity. All of your securities are breaking down, the economy is collapsing, the Shadow government is being exposed, and there is great fear awakening within you, as well as being projected to you. This must happen; as the old structure and belief systems are being shattered, your fear is that you will not be taken care of. Many of the old structures that are collapsing were fear-based and controlled you through fear, through the intention of form. You will experience the shattering of many more of your beliefs, patterns, and perceptions. You will experience many more of your securities stripped from you. It will become even more turbulent before you move out of the collective karmic death of duality. You are in the middle of a hurricane of collective emotions.

As you continue through this collective karmic completion, you will continue to see many of your hopes and dreams shattered, and from this you will collectively move out of the Ego and into a place of surrender into the heart. All must come down to be rebuilt. You cannot put the new structure on top of the old. It must come down, and that is happening now.

The gift of this is that you are awakening. Before this great awakening you were like sheep being herded in the night. Now your eyes are wide open, and you are standing at attention because you have great fear of losing your foundation. That foundation was temporary. If it were not, it could not crumble or collapse. The only permanent foundation is you, with Me.

As I said, you are in a death and rebirth at the same time, and neither one of them is easy. Through this rebirth, you are building a new foundation. This new foundation is I: Mother – Father – God – Creator. You are awakening into the love, light Cells of My consciousness, and together We are expanding you beyond time or any form and into the freedom of your Souls' Song, the love of your Being. Together We will co-create a new world, a new Earth; one of love, light, peace, harmony, joy, happiness, abundance, prosperity, and health for all!

Through Our co-creation, you will soon be walking easily and effortlessly through heaven on Earth. You will not feel separate from Me. We are now merging together as one consciousness of the higher understanding of knowing.

You are moving into the collective heart of love and wanting for your brothers and sisters throughout the world the same as you are now deserving for yourself. You are moving through the birth canal and into the womb of My love.

# Rebuilding a New World – Riding the Waves of Freedom

*"You will experience a great love and appreciation for*
*the simpler things in life together."*

I say to you, "You will rebuild!" This rebuilding will come
from a very conscious place of intention, of humbleness. At
this time, you are still in a place of anger and injustice and are
now taking your power back. The only way you can do this is
for all to be exposed so that you can understand what is going
on in America and your world. That has been done. You will
no longer be victims being led around by false powers. It may
seem like everything is continuing to fall apart; but actually,
you are emerging in a higher consciousness as you continue
to move through your collective emotions.

You will experience a great love and appreciation for the
simpler things in life together. You will not be so wasteful.
You will no longer be a disposable society.

You will be more appreciative of the Planet Earth and
for what everyone has gone through together. You will have
more meaning in your life. You will return to the importance
of family and relationships.

As all of you are being brought to your knees together,
you are seeing each other again and reaching out to one
another. You are rowing your boat together, this boat being
your new intention for your world. You will get through. You
are returning to the true Garden of Eden where you will be
standing naked together. This nakedness is the absence of

your patterns, programs, and old perceptions.

The old structure, or paradigm, must come down to be able to build a new one; that is happening now. With the economy strong, you did not know who you were. You thought you were your homes, cars, boats, TVs, etc. From the collapse you have the opportunity to experience yourselves again, to slow down and feel your hearts. You are now opening up to Me again in prayer, many times on your knees in desperation.

I hear you; I am holding your hand as you continue to walk through your darkest fears. Together We will persevere and move through this false reign of Shadow power, of greed, of too much emphasis on materialism.

You are now filling your Soul with Spirit, with Creation, with Me. On bended knee you are gathering the strength to go on. You are coming together and carrying each other over the finish line back to the heart, back to what is important, to what is real, and that is love. Love is the only truth and safety that there is.

You have heard the song 'Without love you have nothing at all'. This is true. When you are on your deathbed and ready to leave your body, the only thing that will be important to you is love. If you have not had love, you will feel a loss that is unimaginable. You will not be thinking about your homes, cars, or materialism.

Your whole life will go before you, and this will be your judgment day. It is not Me who will be judging you; it will be you judging yourself. What did my life mean? It went so quickly. Did I make a difference in anyone's life? Did anyone love me? Did I love others? You will be in a higher vibration of Me and viewing your life through the lens of My heart and your pain.

You are now collectively in the karmic death, and your life is moving before you. You are now asking yourself these questions. I hear you crying, crying out for love. Where is love in my life? Where is my divine partner? What is my Soul's purpose? I feel like I can't live on the Earth any longer without love or joy or happiness. I feel like I can't live another year like this. I say to you I am with you, and as you continue to open your heart to the heart of Me, you will have love.

You are love; you were created in great love. As you continue to surrender the illusion of love (whi ch is really fear of love) all karmic veils that hold you back from love will dissipate, and in front of you will stand a brilliant mirror of your own love and magnificence. Everywhere you look or turn, you will have and experience love.

If you are longing for your divine partner, he or she will be standing there to take your hand. Your Soul's higher purpose will magically appear to you. You will feel so at one with Sophia's and My love that Our hearts together will open your consciousness to all possibilities of love. Through self-love you will be able to receive the love that you have waited for, that you already are.

It is then that you will be grateful for what you and your world are going through now. You will feel blessed that you had the opportunity to move through the collective "Dark Night of the Soul." You will feel weary and somewhat beat up but in a good way. Your lens of perception will be much higher and you will feel a freedom within yourself that you did not know to be possible.

You will be more integrated with your higher self and the balance of Me through all dimensions. You will know and remember that you are Spirit in a human body, and that you have come to the Earth to experience freedom, and from this Knowingness, you will feel great joy and happiness and will actually be able to laugh at yourself for all of what you thought was so important.

You will feel happy to be alive at this time of transition; you will feel grateful for your process because your life will have more meaning. You will be grateful to be back in the new Garden of Eden with Me and with all of the great Masters in Spirit as well as those on the Earth.

You will have merged through dimensions as one consciousness of love in many different bodies, with many different personalities, in many different color-sound frequencies that have merged together in a beautiful symphony of all Creation. In the new Garden of Eden, you will want to share with one another all of your great gifts. Your consciousness will be higher as will be your lens of perception. You will see through My eyes and heart. You will experience your cup full instead of half empty.

In the future, this is already done. Your job is to continue to unravel what isn't and you will morph into what is. You signed up to be on the Earth at this time. It was your Souls' agreement. You knew all of the losses that you would be going through individually and collectively. You signed up to be on the Earth to experience the greatest time of transition ever and to collectively move out of Karma through the 2012 and all doorways into the 13-13 within yourself and eventually into freedom. You have the opportunity to release all karma and to live your life through intention with Me, to co-create a new life, a New World consciousness and a New Earth.

I want you to breathe in your beautiful future into the now. Feel My words and love for you. Allow your body to take in your new story, your new script, the one that you signed up for, and that you wrote before you came down to the Earth.

Set your intention for this to be, and it shall. Connect your heart and intention with My heart and intention.

Together, We will ride the waves of freedom through all doorways into the 13-13 within yourselves and into Enlightenment and Ascension. You are the ones that you have been waiting for.

**Thank you, and so it is.**

# AWAKENING YOUR
# INNER CRYSTAL CHILDREN

*"The Crystal children are the heart of who I am."*

Many Crystal children are being born on your planet now. Their energies are very high, as they are prisms of pure consciousness. They carry beams of light, which are shattering the collective Ego of fear on your planet. Many of you are these Crystal children.

You are coming into a new lifetime, or consciousness, without physically leaving your body, and your crystal light children within you are disarming your karmic children from old frozen patterns. You are awakening and remembering total consciousness (knowing).

The Crystal children are the heart of who I am. As you look at yourself, you will experience your sensitivity and sometimes what has been thought to be over sensitivity. This sensitivity is the crystal structure of your light. As you are light, you bring, or draw, all to you. Some of the energies that have been attracted to your light are old Shadow frequencies. The Shadow frequencies have a different sound vibration than the crystal light. At the time of your incarnating to the Earth, the frequencies on your planet were not strong enough to hold this energy collectively, and because of this many of you have felt shattered, hurt, insecure, afraid, and alone. As you took this old frequency-sound thought form in, the sound was so dense and different that it was not compatible with your own light vibration. As it hit your crystal energy, it downloaded, or bombarded, you with all of these negative fear thought forms. Because of your crystallization, you took it in and thought it was you.

As you are awakening now, remembering and once again becoming a collective crystal consciousness, your light is so strong that the old fear thought forms cannot penetrate you. Your crystal energy is shattering and dissipating the old frightened aspects of the Shadow. Now the energy on Earth is high enough to hold this crystal polarization. Because this frequency will not allow the Shadow to continue to expand, it starts breaking it loose. You, the Crystal children, were very much needed on the Earth to create this polarization.

Lady Diana was one of the great Crystal Beings who agreed to come to the Earth and open the heart of her country and the whole collective world's heart. She opened a huge light portal, shifting and lifting the whole consciousness into a higher vibration of Creation. This was her great purpose and mission. Had she not been so heartfelt and human in her life experiences, she would not have touched and opened the collective heart on such a level.

You have also had other great crystal beings born on your planet to open the collective heart. In days to come you will see many more of them emerge into the limelight.

Your sensitivity is what allows you to have this great heart connection with Me. It is what has assisted you to continue to search for the Truth, for love. You are the gatekeepers who have agreed to come to the Earth to open the hearts for many. From this sensitivity, you are now bringing this great love and unity to your planet. Can you see that you are creating Heaven on Earth?

Now that you are awakening into this crystallization, you are holding the frequency for the Crystal children who are being born on your planet. They are the future of this civilization. You went before and opened the door for the birth of the new consciousness to become fully enlightened. I know this has been a difficult journey for many of you. I honor you for your agreement to assist this great awakening on your planet.

The seeds of these Crystal children are you. You knew that inside your karmic child is a crystal child waiting to be given permission to awaken, or regenerate, itself to original form.

My gift to you is a collective rebirth of yourself. For those of you who have chosen this difficult path, as you reawaken and realign, you will have the love, happiness, joy, communion, and prosperity that you so desire. You can come back home within yourself to total consciousness. This total consciousness is Creation. As you realign with this Creation energy, you become the Co-Creator of your life and purpose. You can rewrite your script, your agreement on the Earth, for all is energy and you are all. As I AM a Creator Being and you are Me in my highest consciousness, you will be able to use this frequency to co-create your new reality, for you are a Creator Being.

You are the Crystal light consciousness that has been waiting for permission to awaken. Your DNA coding has been activated and your time to awaken and remember is now.

Together through your heart's intention, you are co-creating peace on Earth and a better world for all. You are the ones that you have been waiting for. Welcome home. And so it is.

# INDIGO CHILDREN

*"You are My freedom expressing itself out of form."*

Indigo Children are the warrior children. They are the will, or mind, of Me and will continue to hold the door open for the Crystal Beings. Many of you are great Masters coming to the Earth through the Indigo ray to open the door for the collective Indigos. You, the collective Indigos, could be called some of your flower children. It seems that many of you are dancing to a beat of a different dream. In actuality, you vibrated in a different color-sound frequency. It was and is much higher than the old mind-set of Me. You are My freedom expressing itself out of form.

You opened the door to move you back into the love-heart frequency, not in the love mind-set, but in the love-heart Beingness. You have been on the Earth and other planets that are ascending many times. Your agreement is to bring your vibration into your civilization and to open the door to move you out of duality, out of a time frequency, and into a death and rebirth of a consciousness.

You have had some Master Indigo Beings born who came to change the consciousness of your planet. They opened the doorway for the masses of the Indigos to go through.

Some of your great Master Indigos were Gandhi, Martin Luther King, Jr., President Kennedy, Mandela and Mother Theresa. A major player on your planet in America now is Oprah. She came down to your planet born into great opposition, and as she pulled herself up and out, she, the feminine, opened the door for the collective consciousness to move into a higher vibration.

As you look at your world, you will experience many other Master Indigos. You have had many great masters in your Eastern cultures, such as the Buddhas. Every society has had great Indigos of the light, which have come through to open the doorway for the collective to rise into a higher frequency. Many of the Master Indigos have given their lives to assist the collective consciousness. When they left your planet, they opened a huge doorway of light. This happened because their whole agreement was to assist the collective consciousness to evolve through hope, through the Heart Awakening. Because you are each other, when these Beings, or Souls, left the planet, they expanded an aspect of you with them, which opened a door within you of a higher understanding.

The Master Indigos who left the Earth through assassination had agreed for this to happen. Even if there was a conspiracy behind it, their deaths, or transitions, were supposed to happen. Conspiracy is the Shadow Beingness. The light ones do not conspire to harm or hurt other Beings. The light ones who agreed to make their transitions or go through their Earthly deaths in this way are Master Indigos who have actually risen above the death fear cycle. To them, all is a rebirth, and they agreed to make their transitions in this way to wake people up.

Through such great loss, people, or Souls, want to understand why; what happened? In the search for truth, the veils of illusion, or the Shadow, starts being exposed and the light Souls of you start making healthier choices, for you, your children, your families and eventually your world.

Just as you have had many Indigos go before you and open portals of light, you, the collective Indigos, are now riding these light rays home into freedom within yourself. You are opening the door for other Indigos to awaken into their light and freedom of their Soul.

As you move through the Indigo Ray home, you will find yourself merging with the Golden Christ Ray into a new lifetime without physically leaving the body.

You will feel yourself awaken into crystal prisms of light – into your Inner Crystal Children of a higher consciousness – of all knowing – of Isness into the Second Coming of Christ, the Bodhisattva, the I AM of All That Is.

# LOVING YOUR SHADOW INTO SELF-REALIZATION

*"When your energy of self-love, self-respect, and integrity is strong enough, it will break your own Shadow loose from the collective Shadows' hold."*

My intention is now to assist you out of duality by you experiencing and understanding the Shadow, so that as a nation and world, you can come back with each other as one world under God with liberty and justice for all. The Ego Shadow needed to be exposed and brought to a head, which has been done. You, as a people, needed to understand that the Shadow is its own entity and has a great purpose in assisting the awakening and healing of this planet.

This Shadow is its own entity. It thinks it has a mind of its own. In reality, it cannot exist unless it is connected and supported by the collective Shadow. All Shadows are fear-based illusions and have no power on their own. When many of the fear links are broken and replaced with love, the Shadow starts unraveling. Because it feels and knows it is losing its power, the Shadow will do everything it can to continue to control you. It does not want to lose its grip and is in great fear of its own death.

Your Shadow will try to pull you back into fear and conflict in all aspects of your life. Because the Shadow has been such a great part of your life, it knows your weaknesses, because it has been your weakness. The Shadow will reinforce itself by finding ways to realign with the collective Shadow. It will then try to pull you back into your old patterns.

This is why a Being who has had addiction patterns may have months or even years of sobriety and suddenly finds himself back into the addiction. This Being may say, "I don't know what happened. The next thing I knew I was using again or abusing again." This is true. The Soul may not even know how it happened. The collective Shadow stepped in, took over, and pulled the light Being, or Soul, back into the pattern.

This is why it is so important that as you start remembering your own love, light, and magnificence that you align yourself with the higher frequency of your Soul Group's energy and other Beings of like consciousness. You will then be able to hold the light and frequency for one another. When one of you is in the middle of a karmic wave of emotions, you will have your light brothers and sisters holding the love frequency for you to move through it into a higher vibration of self-love collectively. *Remember, the Shadow has no power by itself!!*

When your energy of self-love, self-respect, and integrity is strong enough, it will break your own Shadow loose from the collective Shadows' hold. Your light and own self-worth and self-love will send shock waves, or frequencies, into your Shadow, breaking loose the old karmic fear-based collective structure. You will then consciously be able to send love and light into your Shadow and break all karmic contracts and programs that are being reinforced by the collective.

As you break your Shadow loose from the collective and resolve old contracts and agreements, you will then be able to retrieve all aspects of your light, love, joy and prosperity, which were vibrating in or being held hostage in duality.

You will always have a Shadow; *the goal is to bring it into the light, into self-realization.*

As you mirror your light consciousness into the Shadow, eventually it will awaken back into love and light. Your Shadow will then vibrate in the self-realized frequency, or consciousness, which will support your light. Your light and Shadow will have arrived together beyond duality.

Your Shadow will become your lights' ally, and they will dance together in love, light, and your Souls' Freedom. Love your Shadow. It is your unconscious part of you awaiting to become conscious.

*"Many feel the light is being put out. It is just the opposite. The lights collectively have become so bright that the flame can no longer be seen."*

Many Beings who are leaving your planet now have agreed to allow this karmic duality to play itself out within them. As they carry this frequency and they agree to leave, they open many passageways for others to follow. This does not necessarily mean that others will physically leave their bodies, but through the emotions of loss, they will open their hearts to a greater understanding of love, of what is important in their lives, and to their inner wisdom.

Can you see that these Souls leaving have agreed to collectively come together to awaken themselves and your planet, to hold the light frequency for all of you, to bring the Earth out of duality? You look around and see much fear.

It is an illusion. You are in a holographic universe that is very much needed so the old fear thought forms and vapors of thought will have a place to dissipate and burn themselves out.

The Christed I AM energy is so high that the light flames are dissipating duality.

Many feel the light is being put out, but it is just the opposite. The lights collectively have become so bright that the flame can no longer be seen. You are moving beyond time where there is only Isness, where the shadow ego becomes self-realized and becomes one with the heart and light of All That Is.

You are on the Earth with Jeshua once again to re-connect with My highest love and light to harmonize beyond fear or duality. That is Jeshua's assignment on the Earth, as it is yours.

As you are moving beyond karmic time, you are merging with your higher self and higher consciousness, and in doing so are lifting the veils for all to have reflected back to themselves their own self-love and light, self-worth and importance. You are collectively remembering your purpose and assignment of being on the Earth.

You are gliding collectively through the golden ray into the core of your own self-love and heart.

Many of you are feeling this golden light magnificence and are bringing these light aspects together as one. This is the collective love light-Christed I AM energy.

Your beautiful brothers and sisters who have agreed to leave your planet are connecting their hearts' love light-Christed energies with your heart and collectively lifting veils, which activates codings in your DNA of the Second Coming of Christ – of the I AM of All That Is – of your Souls' freedom.

*Love – Love – Love – and Love some more. Whatever the question, Love is the answer.*

# FREEDOM'S DANCE

*"You will move beyond duality together and dance together in love, light, happiness, joy and freedom and in Oneness with yourselves, because you are Me."*

You will always have Shadow aspects, but as you love these Souls/Cells that are hurt aspects of yourself, they will no longer have the power to war against you. They will transform their collective consciousness into self-realization. Because you are each other, as this happens, you will have within you all of the great experiences that the transformed Shadow has learned, supporting your light. You will move beyond duality together and dance together in love, light, happiness, passion, joy, freedom and in Oneness.

My intention is to assist you to empty your mind of old misconceptions and thought forms. As you experience your mind emptying, your physical body will experience the release of these old programs, belief systems, and concepts. As this happens, you start healing and become one with the source, or highest intelligence, of the I Am, which is Me. I am a conscious being of light and love. This light and love will expand itself beyond karmic time, enlightening all along the way. This light threads through all Creation, and its agreement is to love all consciousness, including all old Shadow Ego aspects. This love is the heat that melts fear away. Love cannot be melted away, for love is the true vibration. It is the only constant frequency, or sound.

You have agreed to come to the Earth and extend all beliefs, stretch them to the fullest, so they can expand beyond a right or wrong duality perception. You have agreed to expand energetically beyond a time frame experience. Your higher self has agreed to guide you out of duality, or separation, and back to Me in My highest form, back to Our one heart and Soul consciousness of love, back into your OverSoul Matrix of Creation, and into Oneness of all Consciousness into the I AM of All That Is.

Constantly stay connected to your higher self. The more you communicate with your higher self, the more you move into this energy vibration. You merge together as one consciousness and start living your life from Knowingness.

Start your day in your higher self's energy. The more you ask for this connection, the more you will receive it. As you ask you are creating a phone line to the higher consciousness of yourself.

You are your higher self; you are not separate. Your higher self wants to connect and communicate with you. Its agreement is to guide you, and this is its greatest desire.

Your assignment this week:

*Start your day in prayer. Before you get out of bed, ask for your higher self to connect with you. Ask it if it has a message for you. You may receive a message through your mind and think it is you talking to yourself. This is how your higher self might communicate with you. It may also communicate with you through a feeling of Knowingness. Talk to your higher self throughout the day, and when you go to bed at night, thank it for guiding you.*

You are learning a new energy language. It is your Souls' language. The more you ask for the connection, the more you allow yourself and your higher selfs' consciousness to become one.

All veils on the planet are being lifted, and if you had blockages between you and your higher self, they are being dissolved. Continue to ask, and you will receive. It is your birthright to come home on the Earth plane, balanced and supported in your highest light.

Co-create this magical relationship with your higher self, and you will experience serendipity in your life.

# CHANGING YOUR THOUGHTS TO HEAL YOUR WORLD

*"Anything that is not made from My highest consciousness of love is an illusion that cannot continue to hold its form."*

Focus your attention on the light and love within. Do this in all aspects of your life. You can see the cup half empty or half full. I ask that you see everything full of consciousness, full of awakening, full of blossoming, and full of springtime. You are in the springtime of your Souls' evolution. You have been in the winter and are now emerging from not knowing and into Knowingness with your roots and foundation very strong.

In your subconscious mind, you have every memory that your Soul has ever experienced. Go into the core of your light.

This light will activate all old programmings that hold you back from total consciousness. See all in the positive so that you can change your thoughts into the positive. As you change your thoughts into a higher vibration, you align collectively with the sound frequency and vibration of these thoughts. This can instantly break loose any Shadow structure. This is your own gift: to heal and free yourself, to come to the place now of free will, and choose to be the light and love of who you are.

You have great power within yourself, for you are All That Is. You can co-create your own world and the world around you. You are all Creation, and as you become aware, you have the choice to be the victim of life or to rise to victory, through, above, and beyond the illusion.

If you are not willing to change your thoughts, your world will not change. Your inner world will remain small and one of conflict and hopelessness. As you change your thoughts, your inner world expands into the highest consciousness of Me in all worlds, universes, and creations. As you change your way of thinking, you change your way of acting and reacting, which changes the outcome of your choices, which changes the outcome of your life.

This changes the Earth's frequencies and allows you to glide collectively on the light rays of love into Ascension, Enlightenment, and Freedom.

# FREEDOM OF THE SOUL – SELF-LOVE

*"Love will set you free and allow you to come home again inside of yourself. Love is! Love is your Creation, your salvation, and your freedom. Love is your agreement in this lifetime!"*

Love is all there is. Your whole agreement on the Earth now is to return to love. Love is beyond understanding. It is beyond perception. If you perceive love, you are still trying to understand love. You bring relationships, people, places, things and agreements to you in this lifetime that mirror back your old perceptions of what love is from other references or what you call lifetimes.

All of your lessons, or agreements, in this lifetime are to bring you back to self-love, not your perception of love, but back to the heart of love. Your whole lifetime now is to bring you and Me back together as one in harmony.

I want you to hear and know and believe that everything else in your life, every relationship, whether in person form or experience in pattern form is to assist you to awaken to what love is, not your perception of what you think love to be.

This is the lifetime that you have agreed to come full circle, out of any belief, or perception, that holds you back from experiencing, knowing and becoming the Beingness of love. As the Souls'/Cells' agreement is to find and release these old beliefs, the Ego's pattern or agreement is to keep you stuck in this old fear structure.

Remember, all of what is not Love is fear.

Every single relationship in this lifetime you have been in before. No one has done or is doing to you anything that you have not signed up for and agreed to do or go through. Every player or person you are with now, you have been with before. As we are nearing the end times karmically, Beings have been standing in line in Spirit to sign up for these great lessons. Their intention is to reincarnate on to the Earth plane, so that they can free their Souls/Cells from old paradigms, or structures. Souls want to be on the Earth to finish out any of their karmic agreements, to learn and release lessons of duality. The only way one can understand and come out of duality is to have a body.

As you come back together with each other in your Soul Group's song, you will be able to laugh at your own process. There will be no need to take yourself so seriously. Through the Ascension process you are raising your vibrational frequency beyond judgment.

It would be very difficult for the old emotions to surface if you did not have someone of the same vibration and frequency, or song, to mirror them back to you. That is why you chose, before you came to the Earth, your perfect parents, partners, and relationships to assist you in feeling these old beliefs, or perceptions.

Judgment toward self and others comes from a lower time frequency sequence. As you connect to higher understanding, you will experience that there is no judgment, only love for you and your willingness to assist the evolution of consciousness.

When you move into the vibration and consciousness of

love, that is all you will see; that is all you will experience. You will constantly mirror back to others their love and magnificence.

When your love mirror vibrates into a fellow Soul traveler, his old guards and walls start breaking up and dissipating. They start remembering who they are. Old prejudices, hatreds, belief systems, and fears start losing their power. As the structure of the old dis-ease breaks loose, it starts unraveling from the collective pattern. The collective fear-based pattern loses its grip. This has a domino effect. As the Cell/Soul breaks loose from the collective pattern, this newfound experience of self-love connects to the collective love frequency and sends this power of love energy into the collective pattern.

As you Souls/Cells love yourselves, you break a link in the fear pattern. From this broken chain, or missing link, the collective frequency of love can be downloaded into you and into the pattern.

The more you move into Our love of you and for you, the more you experience self-love. The more you experience self-love, the easier it is for your planet's Ascension and enlightenment. When you move into the place of self-love, you experience all as love, even what in the past, you may have judged, or condemned. All is love and is in its perfection.

The power of love can lift mountains, mountains being karmic turbulence. Nothing that is fear-based can continue to exist in love. The love essence, or frequency, will break loose and dissipate all fear-based illusions.

Love will set you free and allow you to come home

again inside of yourself. Love is! Love is your creation, your salvation, and your freedom. Love is your agreement in this lifetime!

# REINCARNATION

*"Remember, you have played every role that one could ever agree to experience, and now you have agreed to come out of all roles into the highest memory of yourself."*

Your Souls' purpose, or journey, is to experience all that a Soul, or Being, could perceive, or understand. When you have all of these experiences, you will no longer judge someone else. Your Cell/Soul will have expanded beyond the karmic lesson structure.

When you reincarnate you will pick the exact parents that you need to download their unhealed patterns into you. After the Soul/Cell chooses the parents that it will receive its foundation, or lessons, from in this lifetime, it downloads the lessons into the Akashic Records before entering the body. When you enter the body with this new contract and have already expanded the contract into the collective consciousness of yourself, you bring that collective memory with you. You may not remember it, but you are already threaded into it.

Because all is you and you are moving into the collective emotional patterns, it becomes very easy to blame others for what needs to be loved within yourself. Anything that needs to be healed, or understood, is you, and the only way it can grow is through love. That love begins within yourself. You cannot truly love another until you love yourself.

It is always self-love. To get there, you need to go through what is not love, the emotional fear aspects of self, to return to love. All that you cannot love are fear aspects of yourself, which have agreed to be in your life, to bring you back to love.

Remember, you chose your whole lifetime: the stories you agreed to play out and every actor or actress in the play. As you really understand this, you will look at these other players with great love and appreciation, for they are the greatest teacher aspects of yourself.

When you are willing to see all as you, a great healing starts taking place. All is you, not just the Shadow, or hurt, but also the love and magnificence. You would not admire or feel great love and respect for another if you did not have those aspects within yourself. No one can tell you a feeling or emotion. You must have the experience to understand. Within yourself are all great experiences.

Remember, you have played every role that one could ever agree to experience, and now you have agreed to come out of all roles into the highest memory of yourself, which is Me and back into the heart, Soul, and arms of love.

You always create your own reality. You mapped out your lifetime and all the experiences you wanted to learn and chose all the great players that you have brought into your life. How can you judge someone else when you asked for them to be a part of your life? You judge them for not being the way your perception wants them to be. In reality, you chose them to come into your life because you knew they would be your greatest teachers. You are blaming them for teaching you what you asked them to teach you.

Remember, to love yourself totally, you must love all that is you. Instead of blaming, remember to ask; "What is it inside of me that I brought this great teacher here to show me?" When you ask, you will receive, maybe not at that exact moment, because you still have emotions to unravel to be able to get to the place of love and acceptance. Go through the emotions. As you do, you will understand the message, or lesson. See all as you, as great messengers of love and light who have come as your greatest teachers to assist you back home into love, collectively.

As you start understanding the lessons and heal from them, you come out of linear time and reconnect with the higher aspects of yourself that already have a great understanding of love. All is love; the rest is the journey your Soul has agreed to go through to bring you back to love.

What you receive from Us is Our total love and appreciation for you. You come to understand with Us that all you have gone through are experiences of awakening consciousness. Whether you understand the course or not is up to how much you allow yourself to go into your emotions, or your veils of illusions. As you allow yourself to surrender into the emotion of the chosen course, you feel closer to Us/ God because at the core of your Being, or existence, We are each other.

There is no such thing as a lifetime that was a failure. All your experiences were meant to be to bring you into a higher understanding of who you are. You go through all the veils of illusion and in doing so, find yourself again.

That self is a great magnificent Creator Being. As I created all that is you, when you realign your Cells/Souls with Me beyond time, or duality, you are also the highest source of your own Creation, for you are Me in the highest.

# MIRRORING YOUR SELF-LOVE
# TO FREEDOM

*"You are always the source of your own Creations."*

You are always the source of your own Creations. If you are in fear energy, you will create many forms of reality to mirror that back to you. If you are in the victim role and angry with Me, being the Creator Being that you are, you will bring many players in the collective consciousness to mirror the victim back to you. As this happens, you will constantly set this scenario over and over again until you are tired of playing the victim. You will then find ways to come out of that role and create another role, or play, for yourself. With each role, or play, that you are in, you will always find your chosen support team on the Earth, which will cheer you on in your role. When you are tired of the role and no longer get energy from it, or perhaps your support team, or audience, is leaving, you will find another role to play, once again bringing your like vibrational team to you because they are you in the same play.

As you cycle through all of your Souls' growth patterns, your classes become easier for you. You go through a graduation into another realm of consciousness. As you move into this higher understanding, you continue to bring to you like consciousness, other light Creator Beings who support your growth and graduation.

You will hold this new frequency of sound and color and draw the same vibration back to harmonize with you. As you harmonize with one another in a higher frequency, this new sound continues to break the barrier to old frozen fear lifetimes, or misalignments.

As you move through this frozen energy, you start connecting to higher aspects of yourself in all dimensions. As your light becomes stronger, it activates old hidden, or frozen, aspects of yourself that were left behind, or stuck, in other plays, or lifetimes, in other dimensions.

I know I am repeating myself, but I want you to know and believe that there is no such thing as failure, only a transformation of not knowing into Knowingness. You hear much spoken of the Knowingness. As you start moving beyond these lessons, you move into the Knowingness, beyond what you could call karma, or time frequencies.

You are coming out of the separation between the male and female, of the heart and Ego, the light and Shadow.

As you are Me and great Creator Beings, you have the opportunity to assist Me to tame the collective Ego through love. Love is the foundation for All That Is. As you continually love and appreciate the Ego and its role in your life, it loses its power and surrenders, or transforms, itself into the light consciousness of self-realization. I love you and thank you for continuing to cycle through your old warrior ways collectively to assist the consciousness home.

When you have had every experience one Soul could possibly have, you will not have judgment towards others. You will have great caring and compassion.

What you will experience inside yourself is peace. When you truly understand that you agreed to go through these lifetimes, the veils of illusion will be lifted. When you came into this lifetime and other incarnations, you came in with amnesia.

You couldn't remember much of your Souls' other experiences. You needed to forget to remember. If you remembered, you would not understand the lesson emotionally. It is only through feelings that you truly understand an experience. Someone can tell you an experience, but if you have not gone through it yourself, you truly do not know.

You can, from your mind, try to intellectualize it through similar experiences, but you will not truly understand until it becomes your total reality. You agree to immerse yourself into an experience to be able to understand another Creator Being's perspective. There are only perceptions based on your life's experience. When you go through all experiences that a Soul can travel through, there are no more perceptions based on experiences; there is only love.

There is much talk on your planet about unconditional love. You cannot love unconditionally if you still have judgment, or blame, towards any other Souls/Cells of yourselves. As you move beyond judgment, you move beyond time and see others' magnificence as yours. As you go through every experience a Soul could travel through and you release any emotional attachment, you move beyond blame, or confusion, and blend with all cellular structures in total love and Isness. Self-love is your birthright and freedom.

Your assignment this week:

*Look into the mirror each morning and into your own eyes, the windows of your Soul. Tell yourself, "I love you. I love you. I love you. You are safe in love. We are now with our real parents, Mother/Father/God/Creator. We are safe with them."*

*Do this again before you go to bed at night. When you get in bed, go to sleep with these thoughts of self-love. Your subconscious will open the door for more love in your life. Remember, everything is a mirror of your own reflection. Love, love, love, and love yourself some more. Love is your purpose, your destiny, and your salvation!*

# SEASONS OF YOUR INNER AWAKENINGS

*"Allow yourself to be in the flow, for you are emerging*
*into a beautiful butterfly with My wings of freedom."*

Your life and body are like the seasons. None are bad or
right or wrong. Life is a continual cycle.

Death and rebirth are your Souls' cycle, as it is the
body's. On your Souls' journey, you will continue through
many experiences. Sometimes your season is one of spring,
where much energy bursts forth with a new confidence, a
new beginning. You experience this as birth. Springtime is a
rebirth, or rejuvenation, of your consciousness. Summertime
is a time of light, awareness and letting go. Autumn is a time
of remembering, of gratitude, giving thanks and forgiveness,
and of assimilating all of the year's experiences. Winter is a
time of deep reflection; a season of introspection, to go within
yourself to truly experience who you are and an opportunity
for great change and setting intentions.

## Winter

In the winter of your life, you are in a reflection cycle. You
have the opportunity for deep reflections, to experience who you
are, what you want in your life and what is important to you.

As you let the light shine into your Souls' awakening, you
will move further into your Souls' purpose.

The winter season of your life is very important. It is when
the greatest changes can take place, if you allow it. As all of

what you believe or perceive is stripped down or away, you actually have a stronger connection with Me.

As you sort out old beliefs of what you call past and set new intentions, great growth takes place. Winter is a time of setting the intention for a new foundation. All is still, and you can start to see more clearly.

As you allow yourself to go into the emotions, honor them, support them, give them a voice and allow them to tell their story; they will start unraveling and releasing. From this release, you will feel great freedom, peace, and a stronger sense of enthusiasm, and purpose. You will have the strength to go forward again.

As you go through this release, your vibration becomes higher.

Every time you release who you are not, you have more room within to experience who you are, and to expand your light into self-love, to all of the beautiful color-sound vibrations of your Soul.

## Springtime

Springtime is a time of new beginnings of joy, happiness, light, and freedom. If you look at nature, you will see that after wintertime, the trees have stronger roots, flowers are blooming, and there is so much life force bursting forth. Birds are singing again. A great awakening, or a birth, of a new consciousness is taking place. Because you have all of nature's elements within you, and your bodies are aligned with the seasons, you will also feel the joy, happiness, new hope, and birth of this season.

Springtime is a time of rebuilding, of action.

Your vibration is higher and you get to rebirth all of your new ideas or perceptions. As you are reconnected to your highest guidance and understanding, the birth of your new ideas will come from within you, the Master and Co-Creator of your intentions.

## *Summertime*

Summertime is a time of light and awareness. You have given birth to your new ideas and consciousness. You are vibrating in your Souls' higher, sound-color vibration. From this higher place, you will continue to draw back to you like consciousness. The sun is shining, and within you, your great inner light connects to the vibration of the sun's vibration.

Many times you decide that what you enjoyed in the past is no longer for you, or you feel that people you enjoyed before, you no longer have anything in common with. These people are not wrong, as you are not wrong. You have grown, and your vibration is different. You no longer have the same vibration or sound-color frequency exchange with these people. Many times, it means you have completed what you agreed to go through with these Beings karmically. As you move out of these relationships, you make room for new relationships and new experiences in your life. In actuality, they are not new. Nothing is new for you in this lifetime. All whom you meet and experience, you have been with and have experienced before. You are here to complete with one another in love.

Summertime is when the light within you has been activated so that you can see and experience all very clearly, not from old fear emotion but from the emotion of love, self-respect, and forgiveness.

## Autumn

In autumn, it is most important to slow yourself down and reflect on all of the miracles of your life, the first being the miracle of birth, and to thank yourself for your willingness to, once again, take on a body and come to Earth to sort out all experiences through your own time cycle. It is a time to look at the growth that you, your Soul, has been willing to go through, to bring yourself back to the awakened, or enlightened, part of Me, which is you.

Thank yourself for being strong enough to journey through what you call time to assist the collective consciousness back into one love-light vibration. Thank all who are in your life for their strength and dedication to assist you to see and love yourself wholly; thank them for mirroring back to you all aspects of yourself that you need to love and accept. Thank yourself for all the great healing, awakening, and self-awareness, which you are now experiencing and for all aspects of yourself and of your personality that are already in full manifestation or bloom of love.

Autumn is a time to love all, to thank all, to look at the year and see all of your perceptions of struggle, and to love them: to love all that is you.

When you continually see all lessons as gifts and thank them, you are then connecting to My highest energy of love and gratefulness. As you connect to this frequency and download it into the pattern, or emotions, it starts breaking them up. This will free you into a grateful frequency.

As you become aware and start giving thanks for the story you have been playing out for so long, the story starts dissipating. It no longer has any power. It unthreads itself from the collective story and frees you to remember who you are, which is a magnificent aspect of Me, playing itself out to the fullest expression, beyond duality, or fear. "Thank You" is a very powerful expression and energy source. It has a vibration that breaks the fear control frequency. This vibration connects to the highest consciousness of Creation. The vibration of "Thank You" goes back to My awakening with My Beloved Sophia. It reconnects to Me after My heart opened, and all I could feel was gratefulness. From this gratefulness, came My true experience of loving all of My Creations of Me. I was able to love Myself totally. From that place, I was able to love you totally because I created you as Me.

Start giving thanks even when you don't feel or believe that you have anything to be thankful for. Again, you will break the stuck energy, and soon you will start feeling grateful, your heart will start feeling more love and you will truly feel thankful. The simple words "Thank You" plug into other Souls' love-light patterns and songs. They no longer feel judged, or ashamed, or feel that they need to protect themselves by being right. They feel seen, acknowledged, and validated by you. As you give thanks for everyone and everything, your energy starts breaking loose from the patterns, and you can then move into the feeling, or true experience, of forgiveness.

You are in a rebirth cycle of a collective love beyond your conscious memory, or understanding, at this time. Allow yourself to be in the flow, for you are emerging into a beautiful butterfly with My wings of freedom. You are the seasons of Creation – you are Me, Creation.

Your "inner" Internet system is truly a consciousness of the divine mind, or a higher mind of Me. You are the seasons of all Creation. Relax now; know that you already are All That Is.

Give thanks for every season of your life, and you will find yourself opening many doors to the higher love and light of your Being. Remember, your seasonal emotions vibrate with the seasons of your planet. As you allow yourself to flow through the seasons within yourself, your higher vibration will start balancing out the erratic weather patterns that you are now experiencing on the Earth. **And so it is!**

# THE CREATOR & SOPHIA ON SELF-FORGIVENESS

*"Your whole existence has been to bring you back to love."*

You are now moving out of the wounded healer and into the Master through self-forgiveness. Self-forgiveness is one of the most important emotions that you can go through. If you cannot forgive yourself for all of the lessons that you have gone through and conquered, you cannot move into the next level of your Souls' agreement of Mastery. To be a Master is to have moved through all emotions individually and collectively and into the freedom of the Soul, into the higher understanding and wisdom of all.

Sometimes it seems easier to forgive others than to forgive yourself.

This is one of the biggest injustices that you have ever served upon yourself. How can you not forgive yourself for the lessons that you agreed to go through; to free your Soul and the collective Soul?

Many of you look at yourself from what you believe other people's perceptions are of you. You judge yourself from your own beliefs (perception) of what you think others feel you should have been or what you could have done differently. These patterns began from the time of conception with your biological parents in this lifetime and were passed on to you. Many other players in your childhood reinforced these patterns to be your truth. Your agreement was to play them out until the pattern became so thin that you could break through it and create a new agreement of self-love and acceptance, for yourself, and the collective.

You must make time in your life to make love to yourself. You love yourself by forgiving yourself. If you do not make time to forgive and love yourself, no one else will. You teach people how to treat you.

Make time to forgive and love yourself every day.

As you do this, you will feel the old stuck emotions start to release and your light, which was stuck in the pattern will move back into you. You will be retrieving aspects of yourself that were still stuck emotionally. This is you doing Soul retrieval for yourself.

*Look into a mirror and into your own eyes, which penetrate your Soul. Speak your name out loud and then tell yourself three times, "I love you." "I love you." "I love you." Then take a deep breath. Breathe the vibration of this self-love into every cell of your body. You will feel the energy start moving through you. Then do the same thing with the words "I forgive you." "I forgive you." "I forgive you." Make sure you are still looking into your own eyes. Take a deep breath and let the energy penetrate you.*

*Do the same thing with "I thank you." "I thank you." "I thank you." Make sure you say your name out loud and breathe the energy of the spoken word into you. Then say to yourself, "I thank you for your willingness and courage to come to the Earth plane to complete all of these karmic lessons. I thank you and honor you."*

*Repeat this process five times in the morning and five times in the evening. As you continue to do this, your subconscious mind will go to work and activate within you your memories of self-love, self-acceptance, and self-forgiveness.*

The wounded healer served you well. Through your karmic emotions, you created a pathway to find your way back to the Master within You. To become the Master is not to control; it is to free yourself from fear of not knowing and into the Knowingness of all Creations. It is to become one with the Earth, the Moon, the Stars, all living life and to vibrate in love, honor, respect, and integrity, and to become the greatest love of your own Soul in physical form.

To forgive yourself is great power; as you do this you will look at all and know there is nothing to forgive. You will see all Souls in their highest glory and agreements. You will hold the love for all to wake up into the reunion of one another.

Call on Me; I will assist you to forgive yourself. I am the Mother of your magnificence, and my love is strong enough to mirror back to you your own self-love and Knowingness. Know that I love you and that I am always with you, and my heart and arms are wrapped around you tightly, protecting you as you move through your karmic hurts, agreements, and contracts.

You are love. You were created in love. Your essence is love. It has always been.

# THE CREATOR ON
# THE IMPORTANCE OF FORGIVENESS

*"Forgive. Forgive. Forgive. Free your Spirit to receive*
*all of the gifts that are the birthright of your Soul."*

I wish to speak to you on the great power of forgiveness. You must forgive to be able to move forward. All unforgiveness is in a past time frame. Living totally in the now, there is nothing to forgive, but if you cannot forgive, you cannot live totally in the Beingness of now. When you are unable to forgive yourself, it is because you are still stuck emotionally in old stories or karmic agreements that you came into this lifetime from which to free yourself. These agreements are a pattern, which threads through many lifetimes and through the collective consciousness of all possessing the same pattern.

The person, or circumstances, that you feel you are still in bondage with has agreed to be a gift in your life, to mirror the lesson that needs to be released energetically. Forgiveness is a harmonious sound frequency that breaks loose frozen energies, which create conflict within you. If you cannot forgive someone else, you are holding a mirror up to bring the pattern, or conflict, to you over and over again until your life becomes a hopeless energy of separateness, illness, or dis-ease. You will experience yourself looking at others with illusional veils of fear between you and your next step of manifesting all your greatness. If you can't forgive, there is an underlying energy that wants the person, or conflict, which you perceive as unforgivable to experience the same pain, or injustice, you feel was inflicted upon you.

You do not have to accept that what was done to you was right, but not forgiving keeps you stuck in an energy that doesn't allow you to bring your own self-love and freedom to you. What you are saying energetically is that you are no better than the injustice that was done to you because energetically you are still stuck in the karmic pattern.

When you are still stuck energetically, or emotionally, with this person, your not forgiving him actually gives him more power because he is using your light frequency as his own.

Are you willing to give up your love, your life, and your highest dreams? Remember, in the larger picture, there is nothing to forgive; you agreed to complete karmically with this seemingly unforgiving circumstance. If your intention is to forgive and you can't seem to release the energy, it is because you are still emotionally threaded together. This threading may be stuck in a past life or lives with this person.

*Imagine these cords in your heart, solar plexus, and the rest of your chakras. Then, call on Archangel Michael and ask him to cut these karmic cords. He is always available to you. This is a great part of his purpose and role. Imagine the cords within you being cut and pulled out by many Masters. Call on Jeshua and Magdalene or the Masters with whom you connect. There is no competition in Spirit. The light Lords and Masters are here to serve you. They are waiting for you to ask for Their assistance.*

*After the cords are severed and pulled out of you, it is most important that you reprogram yourself by asking for Sophia and I, as your Spiritual Parents, to fill you back up with love and grace. Ask Us and you shall receive.*

As you set your intention to forgive, you are sending a higher vibration of light and forgiveness into the memory of the frozen pattern. This light frequency of love will start breaking loose the pattern, freeing your heart to start vibrating in love again; love releases fear/revenge frequencies.

Forgive. Forgive. Forgive. Free your Spirit to receive all of the gifts that are the birthright of your Soul. Come home now. Move out of all illusion and back into the magnificence of your Beingness. If you believe that you need Me to forgive you, then know that you are forgiven and that I love you. Forgive yourself and everyone else. Come home now into the heart of Creation.

We have come full circle and are coming back together as one consciousness of My own Creation of love. This is the time of great manifestations of the group consciousness, of awakening into love. This love will blend you back together in harmony. As this continues to happen, you will feel yourself more alive, awake, and experiencing great emotions of Love, which will move you into total forgiveness of yourself and others. When you truly know from the depth of your Soul that all in this lifetime is by agreement, you must consciously forgive all whom you feel have harmed you, or created an injustice toward you, and all who you have harmed or hurt, including yourself. You will not be able to move forward in your Souls' highest agreement if you are still in judgment or out of balance energetically with all of your great chosen teachers. Most of all, you must forgive Me and know that I forgive you, so that you can forgive yourself. I have nothing to forgive you for, for all is a great Master Plan of Completion. And so it is.

# MOTHER EARTH'S BIRTH

*"The light is like a river. As it flows through you, it flows into all eons of your consciousness, and it will flow into that lifetime that needs to be healed."*

As the light of Me is awakening your planet and all inhabitants on your planet, energies that are not vibrating in harmony are connecting with each other's frequency, and it is creating a combustion/friction, like a shock or short circuiting. That is what is happening and creating earthquakes – abnormal weather patterns - and what has caused the earthquake and tsunami in Asia and Japan and other countries.

As the planet is moving out of linear time, it is ascending back into all consciousness. The consciousness, which has been dormant or stuck in old belief patterns of karma (caste system, prejudice, fear, control, guilt, etc.), is being bombarded with the Central Sun's frequencies. These frequencies are connecting with and pulling your planet out of the old patterns.

Your whole planet and every one and thing on your planet is a hologram of past structures, beliefs, or karma. When the light hits the etheric body of your planet, it breaks loose the karmic threads that have held your planet in duality, conflict, and separation.

The higher intention is to bring everyone back together as one. These seemingly catastrophic events temporarily lift the veil, cleansing the Souls and the sections of the planet out of collective karma. All became one, moving out of caste, or class-consciousness, or beliefs. When this happens, no one is better than anyone else. No one's life is spared because they have more money or better insurance or come from a better caste system or family. All go through similar experiences, and they still have to come back together as one to assist each other to rebuild.

This is a death of a karmic consciousness, individually and collectively. It opens an even greater doorway for Souls to come back home to Spirit, to Me, collectively. The doorway that opens is a birth canal to a higher Knowingness, bringing all back together as one through all dimensions.

Mother Earth is giving birth to a new frequency. As the Earth is moving beyond linear time, her vibration is becoming higher. As this happens, her etheric body is breaking loose, shattering old structures and patterns that thread back to My beginning of time.

All energies, or memories, in her etheric body are sending frequencies back into her physical body. As the etheric body is breaking loose, it is opening doorways, or portals, for all sickness, dis-ease and karma to release itself from her physical body. This is like a dam breaking loose and opening up Mother Earth's womb and sending her through a master cleansing. This happens with planets as well as humans, when all is moving into enlightenment and Ascension.

You will continue to see many more seemingly catastrophic events happen on your planet. Remember all is by agreement and the Souls leaving agreed to play out these end times for their Souls and the collective. These huge collective endings open massive doorways of light, which pull you and your planet into a higher frequency of the Ascension process.

The Beings who left the Earth through this birth canal

agreed to depart. They are vibrating in a collective energy of love and forgiveness and will be holding this love for the aspects of yourself that are still vibrating in duality. These Beings are gatekeepers who are connecting cellularly with those left behind and are pulling the planet into a higher frequency. All who left the planet at this time have agreed to leave so they can assist the consciousness shift.

Many loving ancestral Beings, high spirit Angels, and Masters greeted the Souls who left their bodies, as they exited the Earth through this new doorway. As they were leaving, they connected to their higher selves and OverSouls; this light created a combustion of energy that was so bright and high that they moved instantly into the collective heart and downloaded the light into the area. This light continued to break up the duality, as waves of love started breaking up the dormant collective fear pattern. Because like attracts like, this created what seemed to be more catastrophes and fear. In actuality a great healing and cleansing out of old energy is happening.

Remember, all traumatic experiences on the Earth plane are karma playing itself out. Had your government system stepped in and assisted the people, you would not have broken the old paradigm of the Shadow. Instead, you had and still have the new light vibration of your heart of love. You are now collectively coming together in one world, coming together in the heart, in love, compassion and caring. You are holding hands, and through intention coming together as one to assist one another; people helping people, Souls' awakening and mirroring the light and love to one another.

As a Soul leaves the body, many who are left behind grieve and don't understand, and through this loss, pain, and grief start looking for ways to heal. People, who in the past had no spiritual understanding, start wanting answers. From pain or loss, you change your perspective, or belief systems. Many times, what was truth for you no longer exists. You find a new way of looking at and understanding life.

Everything in life has a cycle. As I spoke before of the seasons, you are coming into a season in which you have not been consciously familiar. You have read about it or perhaps had glimpses of it. It is the season of total awakening and self-realization, of enlightenment.

As I said, in enlightenment, everything is light to you, even the Shadow. You experience all in love and the higher understanding of Creation. You will be vibrating, seeing, thinking and knowing in our higher self's consciousness, which is you. You may see duality but will not vibrate in it. You will experience all as the same consciousness, both the light and the dark, or Shadow, and all shades in between. As this frequency is threading through your planet, around it, and in it, many of you are awakening quickly, going into enlightenment because the frequency of light is plugging you back into your true energy. As the collective Soul/Cell consciousness continues to become enlightened, it mirrors back to all Soul/Cell structures this light consciousness.

Mother Earth is giving birth, and The Harmonic Convergence in 1987 was a large contraction for the birth canal of the Mother to open and expand herself to a new form of life: Enlightenment, Grace.

If the Mother's birth canal opened all at once, you would experience huge devastation throughout your planet. A major emotional cleansing is happening to the Mother, as well as to all of her children, who are you. If the light of Me connected all at once to the highest light of all of you and the Mother, the planet would explode. The planet is still too dense emotionally to give birth that quickly.

The portals that are opening are actually contractions of the Mother as she is opening herself to give birth to a higher intelligence, physically and emotionally. As the new energy of My light is hitting the Earth, it is awakening your planet out of millions of years of vibrating in between dimensions, in illusions.

All dimensions have their own vibratory rate, or consciousness. You and your planet have been threaded through all dimensions, some karmically. Now as you are moving beyond linear time, beyond karma, your frequency is higher, and you are reconnecting to all dimensions and plugging into higher thought intelligence. As this happens, you are experiencing shock waves of light from these dimensions that are downloading their frequencies back into you and your planet.

You are like waves of the ocean continually moving in and out of each other, merging together as one and each time becoming a stronger wave of consciousness. Soon you will be beyond thought understanding and vibrating in the Knowingness of all that is, bringing you and your planet home to vibrate in peace, harmony, and love, collectively-realized.

You are the Souls, or Cells, of the Earth that are in this great birthing process. A collective birth is happening simultaneously. You are moving out of an old cellular structure of separation. As this collective birth is taking place, the walls of this old paradigm are breaking down and you are finding, or calling to you energetically, all aspects of yourself from all dimensions and realities. You are bringing back lost relatives that are aspects of you. Some have been vibrating in another consciousness for eons of time. They got stuck and forgot that they have a genetic light family.

Every time a doorway, or contraction, appears, it activates the collective consciousness into a higher intelligence and Knowingness. When this happens, many Beings all over the planet start receiving the same information, although they may come from different cultures and speak different languages. All are connecting to the light language energy of a higher intelligence. This higher intelligence is a light language that all cultures understand. This energy, or language, connects to the higher collective mind that all on the Earth understand. As this happens, it lifts the whole Earth and collective consciousness into a higher frequency, moving the Earth and its inhabitants closer to the Knowingness of Me.

We are one. We are not separate. We never have been and never will be. You and all were created as Me. You have always been and always will be.

Thank you for recommitting yourself to become one with Me, with yourself. You are resetting your biological clock beyond a time-frequency to realign yourself with My heart-mind-thought process. You need to do nothing but allow My thoughts, or consciousness, and yours to become one, to vibrate together in grace. **Thank You. It is done! It is done! It is done!**

# LOVE IS

*"When you see and experience everything in its own perfection, or divinity, you mirror back to all love and total acceptance."*

There is nothing beyond love. Everything in life, in all dimensions, is leading towards love. Love is the center of all being, all knowing, and all understanding. Your whole karmic process is leading you back to the center of Creation, which is the heart of love. Your whole purpose in this lifetime, or any lifetime or agreement, is to lead you back home to love.

You have gone through a process of elimination. You have constantly cleared veils away, every time becoming a little more aware of what you don't want. As you go through what you don't want and you cannot find any more of your "don'ts," you will be at the end of the cycle. It is then that you can spin around in another direction and start seeing a new dawn, a new day, and a new beginning.

As you move through the mirror of self-destruction into the hole of not love, you usually feel there is no other place to go. It is then that you start reaching out, looking for ways to heal. You start looking in the direction of light. In the light, there is a mirror of your own magnificence and self-love. You may think that perhaps others have come to you, reached out their hands, opened their hearts, gone before you, and opened doorways so that you could see the light at the end of the tunnel. This is true, and yet, these Beings who went before you are aspects of your own light and magnificence that agreed to be the leaders in the awakening of your own Soul and the collective Soul.

They were the ones who signed up to go through the first doorways, or waves of enlightenment. They are aspects of Me, which have agreed to remember My light and mirror this light back to you so that you also could awaken, remember, and unthread your frequency from the backward spiral, or labyrinth.

Keep pushing, walking through old structures, beliefs, mind-sets, programs, patterns, and agreements. You are moving through the veils of illusions. Yes, I see it is very beneficial to continue to move yourself through the emotional healing process. The more consciously aware and lighter that you become, the more you will attract these old patterns. *They are collective, and your crystallized structure will bring them to you again so that you can choose to make a different choice, for the outcome to be different.* As you make a different choice, you release the pattern. An unthreading of the illusion of duality is happening.

The setup looks the same, but the outcome gets to be different.

You are experiencing this happening to all Beings on the planet at this time. The veils are being lifted beyond time and sending light sound frequencies into the collective structure, awakening all consciousness beyond the speed of light into Isness. This is why so many of you can travel beyond time into all dimensions. You are able to travel the karmic time line frequency and back into who you are into what you call past lives, or forward into what you call future lives. You would not be able to do this if you were in a time frequency.

How could one move forward into the future, when in your mind-set, it has not happened? Because you are Creator Beings, as I am, and you exist in all consciousness and Creations as I do, you are constantly creating at all instances of your life. When you look at your planet and feel fear, judgment, or hatred for what you see, you are creating more of that for your world; when you see all in love, grace, hope, and their higher purpose, you are also creating that for your world, for your planet, and for all Beings on your planet.

Your purpose in this lifetime is to play out all of your old karmic agreements. Every time you go through a lesson, or agreement, understand the lesson and move beyond the fear emotions, a light bulb goes on in your mind, and you get the experience. At that moment, you become conscious and have a choice to play out the old scene again or to change the scene.

If you decide to change the scene, you are choosing your own value and importance over the old lesson. You re-program your emotions with self-love and acceptance, which completes the karmic lesson. Your vibration becomes higher, and you then choose a lesson, which forms an agreement that mirrors your newly formed love of self, or self-worth.

You will then bring a new mirror, or lesson, to yourself, and it will always have fragments of the old lesson, so that you can reinforce the clarity of your new intention, or agreement.

This cycle assists you out of the karmic agreements. As I said, everyone who comes into your life is a mirror of you, and when you know this, you can ask yourself what the gift is. When you see these lessons as gifts, you will move very quickly through the emotional karmic agreement cycle. You will even have the experience of the painful emotional feeling, and, at the same time, watch a light bulb go on. You will be the observer watching yourself go through this and will be able to laugh and see the humor, as well as experience love and the hurt emotions. You then have the opportunity to move out of fear and into the Creator Being of yourself.

When you truly understand this, you will always watch your thoughts and know that you are creating at all times. Only now, you will become conscious co-creators of your destiny and the destiny of others and your planet. You will know that everything is choice, and conscious thoughts create change.

From this vibration, you will think something in thought and see it instantly manifest (cause and effect). In the beginning of this, you may try to create a parking place or put out the energy for someone to call you. You think your desire in thought and put the thought out to the universe. The universe picks up the thought like a phone call and energetically re-arranges itself to answer your call, sending the vibration or request back to you. You are co-creating energetically with the universe inside yourself at all times. You are co-creating your existence by moving beyond karmic time and bringing your request back to you, even in physical matter, if the need be. Thought is energy, and you can create anything in your life when you understand the power of thought.

When you truly understand this, you will change your world by changing your thoughts.

# Awakening Beyond Duality

*"When you become aware of the power of your*
*thoughts, you have the power to change your world."*

You are a multi-dimensional Being who vibrates through all Creations simultaneously. There is no past, present, or future. You live all at once. In the future, you are already beyond duality. You have already ascended. You are already enlightened. You are already the Master of Co-Creation. So is Mother Earth.

For the planet and all of its inhabitants of Me to heal and come out of separation and duality, there must be duality. If you do not have duality, how can you know what you need to do to come out of it? You would not even know it existed. How do you know the light if you don't experience the dark? How do you know the dark if you don't experience the light?

All in life, both the light and Shadow mirror you in some way, for you are All That Is. Your agreement to come to the Earth plane is to experience separation so that you could choose love over fear from this place of love. There is no separation. All is choice.

You are the Second Coming of Christ. Jeshua agreed to suffer the illusion of a difficult karmic death, resurrection, and Ascension to reconnect with you and open your hearts and minds to a higher understanding. Because you are each other, you have suffered His death and pain as if you were Him. Over 2,000 years later, you are still suffering His death and pain collectively. I hear some of you say, "How could I ever repay Him?" I say to you, take Him off the cross. It has already been carried. Put it down. He did not agree to come to the Earth for you to suffer. He came to the Earth for you to wake up, to remember your love, light, and magnificence, to remember life is eternal, and that you are Him. You are Him and all that He could do, you can do and more, for you are the grand golden collective energy of Him and his Beloved Magdalene.

As you are the Second Coming, many of you great light ones, Masters, have also agreed to come to your planet and lift the veils of illusion by going through some tragic endings to awaken the consciousness to love. Again, I say to you, "Put down the cross. It has been carried." Experience yourself as Christ in the highest of who He is, of who She is, of who you are, which is love.

Many of you are the Masters who have gone before you, and you have recycled back to become one collectively, to assist this great Ascension and Rebirth.

When you become aware of the power of your thoughts, you have the power to change your world. As you understand this, you will know that no one is doing anything to you that you are not asking to be done.

Life is about love. You are on the Earth plane to remember you are love.

When it is time for you to leave the Earth and you look back at your life, it will not make any difference to you how many cars you had, where you lived or what job you held. The only thing that will be important to you is: did I have love? What was my life about? Did I try to help others? What was my purpose? Did I fulfill it?

I am not saying do not live comfortably. I am saying don't forget your purpose: love, self-love. The more you love yourself, the more love and compassion you will have for others. When you totally love and accept yourself, you will totally love and accept others. You will experience all of life as love because that will be your only essence. Self-love will give you strength and power to accomplish all that you could imagine for yourself and your world. When you are love, you are vibrating with Me in total balance, in grace. You and the universe and I will be aligned in our hearts, Souls and minds. Remember, from this great creation of Oneness you truly become the Co-Creator of your life and world.

You cannot heal yourself or your World unless you surrender into your emotions and move into a place of self-love. Inside of all emotions and elements is total silence and peace. I see many of you afraid of your emotions. Because you live in fear of your emotions, they control you. Anything that you fear has great power and control over you. It has great power because it is siphoning off your energy and life force. You are giving it your power. If you don't use your inner source energy – your generator and your life force – your Shadow fear element of you will. It will use your energy and align you with the collective fear frequency.

I cannot express to you enough how important it is to go into your frozen fear emotions, break them up, and take your power back.

When you are vibrating free from fear illusion, you will not be sick. You will be vibrating beyond the color and sound frequency of fear or sickness and dis-ease. All sickness and dis-ease are fear-based frequencies. Sometimes, this sickness connects to old genetic memories inside of you, of other lifetimes when you carried this fear-based frequency. Because there is no past, present, or future, your body cannot discern the difference, and the fear frequency activates the old dis-ease(s).

As you go into fear emotions, they break up, dissipate, and free you to experience the silence, peace, and grace of your Souls/Cells. You turn on the color and musical pattern of love that vibrates collectively in your etheric body. This downloads the new song of love and self-acceptance into your physical bodies, which starts releasing and healing sickness and dis-ease.

All aspects of you will take this sound vibration of love in, and it will shatter all fear illusions, individually and collectively.

Fear cannot survive in love, but love can survive in fear. Love is! Whatever the question, love is the answer.

*This is great power, and this is how your planet will heal and come out of duality. You are all, and as you see all in their innocence, you will mirror it back to all Creation.*

*Love is and cannot be duplicated, by false light. Love is an energy source, which has a power frequency and song so powerful that it can never be destroyed. It is the highest power of all existence or consciousness. Love is.*

*Your assignment this week is to fill your heart with the Golden Christ Love, then wrap a golden blanket, very tightly, around all fear-based thoughts. Bring this golden blanket into the center of your heart, and you will feel your heart's Christ Love melt all fear away. The fear will dissipate, and all you will feel is the love. Then chant the 13-13 mantra to reinforce the love throughout all of your bodies.*

You are love, and your bodies have a memory of love. Reinforce this memory daily. Change your thoughts to create Love, and you will change your life to one of harmony, peace, and health. **And so it is.**

# LOVE'S GUIDANCE THROUGH THE DARK NIGHT OF THE SOUL

*"Love is the warmth that keeps your Soul alive."*

Without love, you would not survive or live very long. Your bodies would close down, and your minds would become paranoid and frightened. Love is the warmth that keeps your Soul alive. It feeds your cells and gives them life force. Even if you feel you do not have love in your life, you have the higher love of Me and others who are assisting you to awaken to the memory of the love that you are. You have love all around you, even if you are not open to it. Your etheric body picks up the vibration of this love and is sustained by it. Love is the food that feeds your cells, and it is the light connection to Me that gives you the strength to be able to go on.

How do Souls who find themselves in karmic situations that seem unbearable continue to go on? What do they hang onto? There is a love frequency fed through the silver cord, which is your Souls' connection to your body, or the umbilical cord to Me. Remember, you are in My master computer system, and when the frequency in your body becomes dim, alarms go off, and a higher essence of My love of you is sent through the umbilical cord, or silver cord, back into you, your cells and bodies.

For some Souls in these dark situations, it is time for them to come home. They leave their bodies and move through a tunnel of light with a band of angels back into the dimension from which they incarnated. When they know they are safe and have gone through a cleansing, or healing process, they review the lifetime to understand the lessons and the growth that has taken place. If the Soul has evolved and completed its agreement of the lifetime, it moves into a higher octave sound frequency of that dimension or into another dimension totally. Your next assignment is from this higher frequency.

Through all of your processes, or lessons, either on the Earth plane, on some other planet, or in other dimensions, you are always guided. You are never alone. You have a Soul's guide with you that has been assisting you through all lifetimes and agreements. You also have many Masters, angels, and other guides or teachers.

As you continue to evolve and your vibration becomes higher, many times your guides and teachers change. You continually bring guidance to you that matches your vibration. As you continue to move beyond time, your consciousness and that of the Masters and Teachers merge together as one consciousness. There is no separation.

Sometimes Souls do not consciously live through the "Dark Night of the Soul" experience, but they always evolve to a higher plane when leaving the body. There truly is no death, just a rebirth of a higher knowing. You evolve to a higher consciousness.

All Souls who volunteer to go through such an experience are greatly honored by Me. They go through the experience for the collective and to create change for the World. The Souls/ Cells of Me who do come out of the experience are changed forever; they move into a higher vibration, or consciousness, of themselves and have a higher purpose on the Earth and for the Earth.

As their consciousness becomes higher, they connect with other Beings of light with these same higher frequencies of knowing. They collectively open portals of light, which pull you and the planet into a higher vibration.

You and the planet glide through this portal of light releasing karmic energies and contracts, individually and collectively. You then activate higher light color-sound frequencies within yourself. This is the Ascension process.

Just as Souls on your planet agree to go through "Dark Nights of the Soul" to lead the collective into a higher vibration, planets agree to do the same thing. Your Mother Earth's Soul is a great Master Soul and is greatly honored for her dedication to go forward to assist the Souls/Cells/Inhabitants of your planet to awaken and to be a leader of the collective consciousness of other planets.

She is a Master Soul who is healing the Earth and bringing it into Ascension and enlightenment. Just as you in human form need the love-light frequency to be able to exist or live, so does your Mother Earth's Soul. She has gone through many "Dark Nights of the Soul," as many of you have. Her purpose is to assist the collective Souls of other planets and stars to move into Ascension and enlightenment. She is not the only feminine Soul of planets in this agreement. Just as you have many of you on your planet who are awakening in love and light and merging back together as one, Mother Earth's heart is doing the same with the other planets and with her Beloved Father Earth.

As you continue your Souls' journey home within yourself, you will find and feel that the light will be much brighter and grander than the darkness ever was.

This light will continue to guide you into dimensions of love, higher knowing, and magic within yourself that you could not have imagined to be possible. You are multi-dimensional Beings that are moving into the grandest love of all, into the core of your own heart and into your own love throughout all dimensions.

You are coming home into the warmth of your own Souls' love. **And so it is!**

# MOTHER AND FATHER EARTH'S REUNION

*"As you continue to love yourself and move into
your higher aspects, you are the collective wings that
energetically carry this great Mother Planet back to her
beloved Father Earth and into Ascension."*

The male Earth is the partner to the Mother Earth. They work together to bring all Earth Souls back into the light. Their Love Story is strong. They are the total balance of each other. They hold the love, light, and purpose for one another to assist Earth and its inhabitants through the 2012 and all doorways, into the 13-13, and into freedom, enlightenment, and Ascension.

You could say Father Earth is the light body of the Mother. He is her constant heart companion and protection. They are the same planet Cell/Soul that have expanded themselves beyond time to embrace and guide all Souls home again into their own divine partner's heart and into the heart of Love and Creation.

Father Earth is a place where the shattered Soul aspects go who have appeared to have failed their Earthly mission. It is what some on your planet might call purgatory. It is actually a holding planet of the Ego.

These aspects that agreed to hold the Shadow come to the Father Earth planet after transitioning from Earth. It is a place where these Ego aspects have all of the different lessons that they have done to others or themselves constantly mirrored back to them.

The male Earth's Soul is in total balance with My mind, which is self-realized and enlightened. It threads through the heart of My balance with Sophia. Mother and Father Earth's purpose is to mirror their perfect union of love into the light of all others' hearts.

The Mother Earth is the heart of the male Earth, and they work very differently, yet together, to balance all fragmented Soul aspects to return to our highest Oneness, beyond duality. As the Mother Earth is ascending and moving beyond time, she is holding the frequency for Father Earth to also lift his veils for his inhabitants collectively.

The Father Earth has agreed to hold the karmic Shadow energy of My mind, and the Mother Earth is the karmic energy of My heart's awakening. Both planets are vehicles for all aspects of Me, both the emotional and mental, to cleanse old fragmented karmic bondages.

As the Mother Earth continues to move beyond linear time and through the 2012 Portal into Ascension, her vibration is also moving beyond the physical karmic matter structure. She is a crystalline structure, which has been activated. You, the inhabitants of the planet, are also changing and activating your DNA structures into a crystalline form. As this happens, you are aligning your crystalline structure with the Mother, becoming one with her and assisting each other into a higher frequency sound, of love, and light. You then realign with Me, the crystalline structure of Creation.

For the Mother Earth to be totally in the balance of love and harmony, she must also be at one, or realign with, her male aspect. For her to be able to do that, she must turn her vibration up, as she is doing, to move into another frequency or dimension, as her male is not in a physical/matter form. You, the inhabitants of Earth, are assisting her in this transition.

Everything is changing frequencies. This 2012 DNA time code awakening is not just happening on the Earth. It is happening in all dimensions.

The Mother Earth is a hologram of Me that is opening and awakening the heart of many of the fragmented aspects who have tried to stay in control. The Father Earth is also a hologram of Me where the Spirit aspects that could not find their way back to Me on the Earth, come to heal. The Father Earth is not a place of punishment. It is a place for the Shadow to realign with the heart of the Mother, to break the old mind-set of fear.

My telling you this story is leading up to the re-emergence of Mother Earth and Father Earth. For the male and female to be in balance, they must come together as one. Many of you on the Earth plane are now separating from and leaving old karmic structured relationships and are coming home with your own twin flames in physical form.

You are moving through the old illusions and veils, awakening into a higher frequency, and moving back together through time and into the arms of your beloved. Mother Earth is doing the same thing. She is moving beyond time through the veils of illusion and back together with her partner, Father Earth. Because their vibrations were different, they could not have vibrated together in their love sound frequency until both cleansed the old karmic structure, or what you could call collective lifetimes.

Just as the planet is moving beyond time and into the higher aspects of herself, you also are journeying through all veils of karmic illusions and reconnecting or merging with all aspects of yourself interdimensionally.

When you have moved through the veils, you and your twin

flame partner will vibrate in your Souls' songs and sounds and make beautiful music together. Mother Earth and her Beloved Partner, Father Earth, are going through the same thing. Their Souls' songs are now calling them back together, lifting them into the same frequency, so they will merge together as One.

When the Earth moves through the 2012 Portal at precisely the twelfth day of the twelfth month at 12:12 A.M., she will merge back together with the etheric body of her partner, Father Earth. This union will be a climax, a completion of the Soul for them. It will no longer be just the Mother nurturing her children. She will be aligned with her Beloved, and together they will be in perfect balance. The frequency of their love together will create such a balance of your Earth that the sound of their Souls' song will start disintegrating the fragmented Shadow.

Mother and her Beloved partner are already vibrating together in other dimensions. They have already reconnected as one. It is in this third-dimensional perception, or reality, where they need your continual love and support. As you continue to love yourself and move into your higher aspects, you are the collective wings that energetically carry this great Mother Planet back to her Beloved partner and into Ascension.

# COMING HOME

*"You are now on the Earth plane to co-create
heaven on Earth"*

You are now in the highest consciousness frequencies of yourself in which you have ever vibrated. You have within your total memory and recall, if you choose, all consciousness. Your Soul has traveled through every experience a Being could possibly go through. You have been All That Is. You have played every role that could ever be imagined. You are now in the greatest show, or production, that you have ever agreed to go through. You have within your memory and experience all of the lessons, individually and collectively, that a person, or Soul, could possibly experience. Now is the time you have agreed to remember the emotions and feelings of these experiences and agreed upon lessons. The setup of your lifetime or story looks the same, but the outcome gets to be different. The outcome gets to be freedom.

You are now on the Earth plane to co-create Heaven on Earth.

You are great, enlightened, Ascended Master teachers who have agreed to lower your vibration and come to the Earth to have a human experience. Because your DNA is being activated, many of you are remembering who you are. This memory is opening and realigning you with the collective, enlightened, Ascended Masters throughout all dimensions.

As this happens, your ideas and perceptions of life change. You want for others what you want for yourself, not in codependency, but in the larger picture of the collective purpose. You move out of the I/Me and into the I/AM. You become more interested in the health and healing of others and the planet. From this place in the core of your Being, you feel and experience your Souls' greater purpose: to become one with the total balance of love with your inner Male and Female, to align with Mother Earth and her divine partner Father Earth, to move through the 2012 doorway collectively, and into the 13-13 within yourself and into ascended, enlightened Oneness.

The 13-13 is the completion within yourself where all twelve of your lifetimes in your karmic wheel come together in one consciousness. You bring all higher selves of the wheels together into the higher vibration of your OverSoul. All higher selves are merging together as one in the center of your karmic wheel. They are transmuting all of your learned knowledge into the higher vibration of the Second Coming of Christ.

You are merging together with all twelve aspects of yourselves into the center of your karmic wheel creating the number 13.

Jeshua has merged together with all twelve of his apostles (his spiritual team) that were on the Earth plane with him creating the number 13.

This is the 13-13 doorway of the Second Coming of Christ within yourself and the collective.

You may not consciously have a memory of the 13-13 doorway, but within you it is being activated.

*I ask this week you continually chant the number 13-13 into your heart so that you align your heart energy with Jeshua and Magdalene.*

*As you chant the 13-13 into your heart, you will actually feel your heart opening to love. You will feel this love move through all of your bodies, filling you up with the golden nectar of the Second Coming of Christ.*

Jeshua's and Magdalene's home is in the 13th dimension. The 13th dimension is one that is a portal through all dimensions. It is a time portal frequency where Christ and the Masters who work with Him can vibrate through all Creations at once. The Christ dimension had to be close enough to your Earth for Him to be able to assist and monitor the Earth at all times and also for Him to have a high enough frequency to move you through and beyond all dimensions.

Jeshua has a crystal temple in the 13th dimension that He shares with His beloved Mary Magdalene. There are also crystal cities in this dimension that were created through thought. The crystal cities have many color frequencies that thread into your planet and through all dimensions so that the dimensions will vibrate in harmony.

It is from the 13th dimension that the crystal cities that are being placed around your planet were formed. They were created in thought and strategically placed over the unbalanced cities on your planet. Just as We are one with you and assisting you in your Souls' awakening, cities have a Soul, or consciousness, and the crystal cities are holding the light for the Earth cities to evolve and awaken.

The 13th dimension receives its life force from the Central Sun's energy. The Central Sun is the generator source for this dimension's consciousness to build the crystal cities. Jeshua and Magdalene are the light ones who have agreed to bring your planet into Ascension and enlightenment, He has agreed, with

His team, to assist your physical bodies and their DNA into crystallized form. Mother Earth is a crystallized form, which is also vibrating this crystal frequency to you … The Christ frequency is the Golden Ray, and this is the energy in which your planet is now vibrating. The generator for that source is the Central Sun's Golden Ray. Jeshua and Magdalene's bodies are this crystal golden frequency. They vibrate in this frequency at all times and are able to hold that frequency for you and your planet.

You are actually riding the 13-13 wave into Enlightenment and Self-Realization collectively with other Masters. You are holding that wave open for all to remember that you are the Masters, Co-Creators.

You are now coming home within yourself riding the 13-13 wave into Freedom.

# Rethreading Your DNA

*"Your threads of DNA flow through all forms of Me."*

Your bodies are a divine blueprint of Me. It may not seem like it to you because many of you on the Earth plane have imbalances in your physical, emotional, and mental bodies. As you continue to unravel the karmic veils of illusion, your body will once again purr like a fine automobile. Your bodies are divine programs, or you could even call computers, which were created in perfect harmony with Me through all Creations of Me.

You are a program that is very much alive. How could you explain your bodies: hair, teeth, reproductive, and other organs? Where did they come from? How does your body know what to do? How does your body know the different cycles that it goes through? After birth, you go through adolescence, young adulthood, middle age, and then full-bloom maturity. Your body also goes through the different cycles of emotions connected to the appropriate ages. Your body eventually goes through a completion cycle and releases the Soul back to Me. You call it death. I call it birth. You go through an ending cycle of your life on your planet and into a rebirth of your light, love, and innocence beyond a time frequency.

Look how your bodies have evolved through time. Your life span is much longer now because your vibration is higher, and you have more of a conscious connection with Me. You used to see Me or experience Me outside of yourself, and now you experience Me as you, or you as Me. The veils are being lifted, and you are remembering who you are. You are reconnecting with and remembering each other in physical form. The veils are being lifted between you and the memory of Me. You are now co-creating Heaven on Earth with Me.

You are a beautiful instrument, which vibrates in heavenly song. As your DNA is continuing to be activated, your song is becoming even more beautiful.

*"You are actually a biologically perfected race of My highest consciousness. You are blends of many colors, sound frequencies, and vibrations that resonate with Me throughout Creation."*

Your race has a very high-level DNA system, which holds total consciousness. You agreed to come to the Earth plane to assist all consciousness out of duality and back into Oneness. How could you possibly do this great task if you did not have all of the tools within yourself? You are collectively bringing the unconsciousness back into the light.

You come to the Earth as a Soul, yet you carry within your DNA the collective consciousness of all understanding of the highest light consciousness as well as all Shadow conflict. You are All That Is. You are the highest vibration and consciousness of any race that has ever inhabited your planet. You have lived every lifetime, every emotion, and every understanding of all that was and is needed to bring the collective back to Me in the highest form. Because you are each other, as you do this, you are rethreading all Beings of Me, who are you, back into Oneness.

You are a collective consciousness, which is assisting each other to assist Me to bring all out of separation from Me. Some of the information within your consciousness and DNA is from the collective. It is not an actual experience that your individual Soul went through. You received the information from the collective Source. Because you are each other, the experience is almost as grand as if you actually experienced it yourself.

Your bodies are very sophisticated Internet systems that are plugged into each other. If you have a memory of yourself in a lifetime where, perhaps you were crucified for your spiritual gifts, your cellular Internet system will open up all websites within the collective and align you with everyone else with the same experience. You will then carry every memory within yourself of all who have been tortured, or killed, for their spirituality. This is why many past life practitioners can take you back into the same lifetime, and you may have many different experiences or outcomes. One person may tell you that you were a man in that lifetime, and someone else might see that you were a woman or a child. You may have one person tell you that you were a man in the Holocaust; someone else may tell you that you were a woman or child.

You may actually have been in that lifetime, but because you are a collective Soul, you experience the memory of many different aspects of yourself at the same time. You may also be connecting to the collective experience of the lifetime and releasing it for the collective.

What is really happening is that you are connecting to the collective memory of the experience. As you release the emotions of the lifetime or experience for yourself, you are breaking the pattern loose for many. When this happens, you actually go into the collective website and break loose the pattern for the collective.

This also happens in the highest, or light, lifetimes. As you awaken into these lifetimes, the websites go on in others and activates another level of light in their DNA. As you go back into light, ascended lifetimes, the same thing happens; you activate the collective, ascended, enlightened websites and assist the whole collective into another level of light.

You are aligned with the vibration of the planet's energy because you are at one with her, or as I spoke to you, you are the Cells of the planet. Every time the Earth goes through a light portal, or veil, you, as a collective, have the same experience. As Mother Earth's website turns on, she also assists other planets and stars collectively into a higher vibration. She aligns herself with other planets and stars that have already ascended and rides on their waves of light consciousness into a higher frequency. She also assists the planets and stars that are not as conscious into a higher wave frequency, for all is One. This Oneness of you is now rethreading your DNA through the 144 dimensions in your Universe and beyond, through all dimensions of Creation.

You are collectively bringing the unconsciousness back into the light. Contrary to many projected and channeled beliefs, this is happening. If it were not happening, your Earth wouldn't have so many conflicts going on. Your Earth is a hologram, which has played out many end times, ends of civilizations, and ends of karmic duality. Just look at the human species now and how it has seemed to evolve through perceived time. Do you not think that I had a hand in this? I allowed and assisted many other species to go to the Earth to evolve their consciousness. Some did evolve and others' Egos betrayed them. Others played out the last of their karmic agreements and left.

Your race has a very high level DNA system, which holds total consciousness. You agreed to come to the Earth plane to assist all consciousness out of duality and back into Oneness. How could you possibly do this great task if you did not have all of the tools within yourself?

You came to the Earth as a Soul, yet you carry within your DNA the collective consciousness of all understanding, of the highest light. You are the highest vibration and consciousness of any race that has ever inhabited your planet.

You are coming home collectively to create Heaven on Earth in all life forms.

# BLENDING ALL RACES INTO THE LANGUAGE OF LOVE

*"Your threads of DNA flow through all of My forms."*

There is much confusion on your planet as to who you are and where you came from. You are actually a genetically threaded race. Your threads of DNA flow through all forms of Me.

Look at all the races on your planet and all their different cultures. Each culture has different tastes in food, clothes, music, religion, and belief systems. Some of your cultures feel more in their bodies; they move with the Creation of Me, and they feel that their Souls' song and Mine are very much in harmony. They sing, dance, and vibrate with the music of Creation. Their dance is a constant recreation of their life force.

Others on your planet experience Me more from their heart and do not allow their bodies to experience or express their Souls' or cultures' song or music. Maybe their religions have told them that it is a sin to allow their bodies to experience joy, happiness, and freedom. Even though they do not experience Me through their bodies, their hearts are very open, loving, and honoring of Me.

Some cultures experience Me totally outside of themselves. I am an understanding in their minds, many times a God of fear and control.

Other religions and cultures control whom you can love and what you can believe in. I see many cultures and religions on your planet that are so afraid of the feminine power that they do everything they can to oppress it, suppress it, deny it, and even crucify it.

The feminine is the source of power! The feminine is what opened My heart and gave me My true sense of power. This is when I came into balance with Myself, when I started creating from My heart. I experienced love. My vibration to create was higher, and I started creating many beautiful colors and songs, which are you.

As the veils are being lifted and you are remembering who you are, I hear many of you say, "I'm not from here" or "this is my first lifetime on this planet." In essence, this is true. Many of you are from other planets, star systems, galaxies, and even universes. You are a long way from home. Your seeds of origin are from other Creations.

I spoke to you before about the Earth being a hologram and that you are aspects of Me that need to evolve and free yourselves from old belief structures.

You have come to the Earth as a collective consciousness of your people from your planet of origin. You are the seed from your planet that is here to seed with others, to heal the rift between consciousness and cultures.

The reason you all look so different is that your DNA structure and physical traits are from the people of your own planet. Now on the planet Earth you see many cultures blending together. Many races are marrying with one another. This is the divine plan. Eventually you will have a blend of many flavors, colors, songs, and music.

You are blending your music together, blending your Souls back together as one. You are blending yourself back together in one language of love.

As I speak of the feminine, I do not just mean a feminine body. Remember, you have been All That Is, and even the male carries the feminine DNA. The more you move into the heart of the feminine love collectively, you open the door to the feminine in all.

The reason you have so many men on your planet who are gay is they have had many lifetimes as a female, and their hormonal systems are sometimes much more feminine than male. You also have the same thing happening to the feminine. This is what you could call a gender crossover. The purpose of this is to bring the Souls on your planet out of gender and back into love.

When you are back in Spirit in the highest, you are not a gender. You are a Soul. You are love.

You are now on the Earth plane to experience and express love for one another, regardless of what gender you are.

When those in Spirit look at you, love you, support you, and assist you, they do not see you as you would. They can see the form body, the home, in which you are residing, but that is not their experience of you. They experience you in your Souls' highest essence: love. We/Me/They/Spirit experience you in your totality of Me, in your higher self, in your OverSoul, and light body consciousness of Me – of love.

It is now time on your planet for the feminine to be unleashed and released for the planet and its inhabitants to heal. This is happening now. As the vibration is becoming higher, it is awakening the feminine feeling in all. The planet Earth herself is the feminine, which is holding her heart open unconditionally for all. The feminine is all-forgiving love.

As you continue to balance your male and honor your

feminine, you will do the same for others. You will see them in their magnificence and hold the love and light for them to see themselves in your mirror of them, in the mirror of love.

Your agreement is to awaken into love, to hold this love ray for all to remember their own self love. You have many Beings of light from Spirit and from your planet of origin that are holding the love and light for you as you are holding the love and light for others. You are not alone. You never have been. You just forgot.

You have always had your high spiritual team and guidance assisting you to awaken and remember your Souls' higher purpose and mission: self-love. Remember, whatever the question, love is always the answer.

# OverSouls and Light Bodies

*"The OverSoul is a consciousness, or understanding,
which vibrates above a Soul's contracts, or agreements,
of evolving."*

Jeshua and Magdalene are the OverSoul for the collective of you on the Earth. The OverSoul is a consciousness, or understanding, which vibrates above a Soul's contracts, or agreements, of evolving. The OverSoul is holding the larger picture, or the energy pattern, above and beyond all lessons. Even planets have an OverSoul, as well as you, the individuals.

Each individual has an OverSoul, which is the orchestra leader, or vibrational sound energy, that holds the vibration of love and light in place for the Higher Self. The Higher Self is the Soul's guardian and connection with the OverSoul for the lifetime, or consciousness, in which you are vibrating. The OverSoul and Higher Self continue to thread light into your cells until your Soul reaches the frequency to be able to expand its energy through the understanding of all lessons.

Every Soul has its own song, and when brought together with other Souls' songs, a beautiful melody or symphony takes place, healing the collective Soul group in which you are vibrating. This Soul Group's song brings all Souls in that particular group together to harmonize beyond the collective karmic agreements. You are then threaded together in love and light, spreading your energies multi-dimensionally through illusional time and back into your Soul Group's OverSoul.

As this happens, you start connecting with, or threading

into, other dimensions of yourself, releasing the veils of separation and coming close to each other's hearts. You will actually feel your heart more open, many times through tears of awakening. You will experience more love, compassion, caring, acceptance, and forgiveness of others. This happens because you are looking through and experiencing through your heart, instead of your mind.

You can only give to others your own experience of love. As the collective is holding you in harmony and love, you begin to mirror back to others their innocence, harmony, and love.

All is love. You are in a continual cycle of moving back through karmic time frequencies and into My heart's sound of love. The OverSoul plays a big part of this process. Without the OverSoul, you would feel lost. Your OverSoul is your guiding light back to Me. It carries the highest frequency of your Soul's sound. You continue to follow the sound through many dimensions and back home.

As you move through the veils and reconnect with others in your Soul Group's song, your collective vibration connects you with your Soul Group's OverSoul. This is why many of you are so happy to be reconnecting with others of like vibration, or consciousness. You are back together with your Soul family. You feel great love for one another and feel like you know each other. You feel this because you do. These Souls are you who are mirroring back to you love and acceptance, your Soul's song. You don't feel judged. You feel loved, which creates a vulnerability because the veils are gone, and there is nothing more to hide. They really see you and love you in totality of who you are.

When this happens, you know you have moved through

much karmic patterning and are coming back together in your love and innocence.

As you expand further into your own self-love, you and your higher self integrate more as one self. As you and your higher self integrate more as one self, you expand further into your OverSoul. Eventually, you will expand back into the heart of Me, the OverSoul of Creation, which is you in your highest, most eloquent form.

# LIGHT BODIES

*"Your light body is the highest expression of your light form. It is beyond time and vibrates with Me in My highest consciousness of love, light, and sound."*

How is the light body connected to the OverSoul? The light body is the vibration of the OverSoul's consciousness, or you could say the etheric body of the OverSoul that is totally conscious. The light body extends from the OverSoul and connects to your etheric body. It is what gives your etheric body the energy to vibrate and it keeps you connected to the OverSoul.

Now as you are moving out of linear time, you are vibrating with and becoming more aligned with your light body. Just as the OverSoul guides your Soul, the energy of the light body connects to your etheric body and guides it. Now you are merging with your light body, just as the Earth is merging with her light body.

All is energy. Your light body is the highest expression of your light form. It is beyond time and vibrates with Me in My highest consciousness of love, light, and sound.

As you are moving through all dimensions and realigning with your light body, you are hearing all aspects of your own frequency in these dimensions. Remember, all is you. You may hear sound vibrations, which seem dense, but as you readjust your thinking, you will hear the sound pitch readjust itself into a higher frequency. This is your own vibration merging with and being guided by your light body in and out of duality, or your Shadow, back into the light.

Your guiding light, which is your light body, your etheric body, and your physical body are vibrating together, creating a combustion of light sound that activates the lower sound vibration within all of your bodies: the mental, emotional, physical, cellular, and etheric bodies. All of the emotions vibrating in the lower sound frequencies are being activated, and there is no place for them to go but up and out.

Release them. Thank them. Love them and let them go.

This is how you heal the world by healing and loving yourself. As you and your light body vibrate together, the sound frequency is so high that it breaks loose the karmic collective emotions from your bodies and systems. When this happens, you unthread from the collective pattern in your etheric body breaking its structure loose. You are merging with your light body into Ascension. Your light body also is aligned with the collective light body.

Many of you on the Earth plane are experiencing a great shift of your own frequencies, or consciousness. You are not just intellectually verbalizing that you are one; you are actually experiencing it. You are vibrating in a higher vibration, or caliber. You are seeing the world and your brothers and sisters through a different lens. You are feeling more love for All That Is, and instead of going into old thoughts of fear, or condemning, you feel more love and compassion and see more of the divinity, or higher consciousness, of this shift.

When you are in alignment with the Me in you, you will emanate a light so bright that it will warm your world. Your world will feel warm from love.

This is the time that your Soul has waited for. Souls are lining up in Spirit to come to the Earth at this time to move through this incredible shift – through all dimensions and into the freedom of the Soul.

Having love, empathy, and compassion for others does not mean that you will give your power to them. It is just the opposite. You will love yourself enough that you will be able to hold love for them unconditionally but will have no fear of them because your fear-based emotions will be loved, healed, and freed. **And so it is.**

# MOTHER EARTH'S LIGHT BODY IS RETHREADING WITH HER BELOVED MALE PARTNER

I am reminding you that there is no past, present, or future. Just as you have already ascended and become enlightened in the future, so has your dear Mother Earth. You are from the ascended consciousness, which has come back to the Earth to assist others and the planet into their Ascension. You and other light ones have followed your frequency back in what you call time to rethread the collective consciousness into their higher self-expression beyond time.

As I spoke to you before, many have seen the Mother's light body, for she is merging back to her beloved male partner, and their heart frequencies are vibrating in a frequency of love that is breaking all old karmic sound barriers to frozen emotions and grids of the planet. This union's vibration of love is so strong that the heart opens up and draws the light body, not only around the planet, but also into it. As the Earth is a hologram, you could say it is three-dimensional. The light body threads through all dimensions, through the grids and meridians of the planet, and into the core of the Mother's Soul; this is happening now. The light body and the physical body of the planet are starting to merge slowly, as the heart and Soul of the Mother and Father are reconnecting beyond a time frequency.

As the Earth is shifting on its axis, it is shifting the Shadows' hold and breaking loose the frozen emotions, or consciousness, that is stuck in the grid system of the planet. This grid system threads back before the Soul of the Mother Earth was lifted here from Maldek. Not only did the Soul of the Mother bring much with her karmically that needed to be healed, she also agreed to take on and cleanse all karma from the body of this planet's collective consciousness. This shift has needed to happen slowly because there was so much history and density in the grids that a super consciousness of light would have blown out the crystalline structure, or electrical system, of the planet.

Now that the Earth has shifted on its axis and released dark vapors and poisonous gases from her structure, there is more room to hold the light. The light I so speak of now is the light body of Mother Earth. As I mentioned, many of you who are ascending and are consciously experiencing yourselves in other dimensions have seen the light body of the Mother. This light body wants to be seen and even photographed. The light is very high, and the more visible this body becomes, the more it lifts the vibration of your planet and all of the inhabitants. What one is actually seeing is the mirroring effect of the light hitting Mother Earth's crystalline structure and vibrating back to her crystalline light body.

In the future, Mother Earth has already ascended and is already enlightened. She has already moved through the 2012 Portal, back together with her beloved Father Earth, and merged with her light body and OverSoul.

I wish to tell you again that you are not going to lose your planet. She is already home. This does not mean that you don't have to continue to grow and heal. You must, so that you can hold the light for her and yourselves to move from the past, into the present, to shift the future, to co-create Heaven on Earth.

I have spoken to you much about your thoughts. Thoughts have great power. You are the Co-Creators of Me. Know that We are already one with all consciousness, for all is Me. Together, let's co-create through intention, a higher consciousness for a harmonious world so that all can live in the Garden of Eden, in Grace.

Thank you. It is done. It is done. It is done.

# AWAKENING STARGATES AND TIME PORTALS WITHIN YOURSELF

*"As you continue to move beyond time and through the portals opening up for you, you will find yourself merging together through these stargate portals."*

There are many stargates on your planet that were formed through thought and solidified into form.

The stargates are in geometrical alignment with the meridian lines of Creation. Many Beings of the highest understanding of Creation partook in the forming and creation of these gateways.

Different stargates have different purposes. You have major gateways and smaller ones that were created by many of the Beings of light, which had incarnated to your planet. The smaller ones were created to be the activators of the larger ones. The smaller stargates were created from the same architectural design as the larger ones. The designs were given to many Beings on your planet whose agreement was to protect the larger gateways, or stargates.

One of the reasons there is such a great interest in your planet Earth from other Beings, Souls, and life forces, both light and Shadow, from other planets is because of the stargates.

The largest stargate is the one under the Giza pyramid in Egypt. There is much interest in this one because it is a time portal gateway that is generated by the Central Sun's energy. This time portal gateway runs through the universe's grid system. It is used as a passageway back and forth through any time zone consciousness. This stargate moves you beyond karma. Karma is in a time frequency. Beyond time, there is no past, present, or future.

You could experience that much of the galaxy and universe in which you are vibrating, goes in and out of time. When one understands how to use time, or you could say to manipulate time, you could create whatever your thoughts think instantly. You would know everything simultaneously. You could create an instant thought manifestation into form.

The time portal stargate was designed to assist the light ones, which are many of you, to move very quickly to destinations. This was so that the Creation would be able to expand its consciousness out of time and back to Oneness very quickly. This was not to manipulate time but to move beyond it quickly, to be able to assist all sounds-songs frequencies to harmonize and blend in love and light. The time portal takes one instantly through time, through illusion, and back to truth into Knowingness. All light would go on simultaneously.

Many of you light Masters have great understanding of the stargates. Some of you even helped design and build them. You are now back on the Earth plane to protect them, your worlds, and the Souls, or species, of your worlds. The only way the stargates can be activated is for the highest golden love frequency collectively to harmonize. That is what you are doing now as you are moving out of duality. You are etherically moving through these gateways beyond linear time and reconnecting with yourselves in other dimensions. If some of the selves still vibrate in the Shadow, your own collective love and light is so high that it is disempowering your own Shadow and bringing its light back into you. You are re-emerging with self individually and collectively. From this like love-light frequency Song, nothing can penetrate you that is not of the same Song.

## China Stargate – The Heart Chakra

The China stargate is the second largest. There is a stargate underneath the pyramids in China. Yes, there are pyramids in China. It is the feminine stargate. Is it not interesting that in China the feminine has been so oppressed, and yet, it is the country that holds the gateway to the heart? This stargate was created by Beings of Me who have ascended beyond any male or female aspect, and their hearts, minds, and Egos support each other in beautiful song. They vibrate in total Knowingness. We vibrate together in perfect harmony.

This gateway is in direct alignment with the heart of Mother Earth and with the heart of other planets and star systems. Just as you Souls/Cells on your planet have come back together in the heart with one another, so are the Cells of Me who are planets. The heart stargate in China is in direct alignment with the meridian system of the Central Sun's energy and in alignment with the grid systems of all central suns back to the center, with My heart, with My Sophia.

The heart stargate vibrates in total love and balance of My heart. It is aligned with the hearts and Souls of other planets that are in this great universal awakening.

Once the heart stargate is activated, it will open the hearts of the Souls/Cells of you in your world. As this happens, there will be a simultaneous opening of the other gateways, such as the time portal in Egypt. This Egyptian stargate is in total balance and is holding the strength for the Heart stargate. The only way any stargate can be opened is through love, or the collective vibrating in a heart octave, or sound frequency, which resonates with the coding in the etheric electric system of the stargate. The stargate's etheric body system is a sound system. It can only be opened through a harmonizing frequency equal to it.

Because you are each other, as your Cells become conscious enough, you thread into each other and start sending the healthy balanced love into the Cells, which have been more dormant. You see this happening all over your world now. Souls/Cells are vibrating in a higher octave, or sound, than ever in your Souls' history. You are blending your Souls into a symphony of color and light that will eventually open the stargate.

### Peru Stargate - The Root Chakra

There is a very powerful stargate in Peru that is the root chakra gateway.

This stargate runs through the underworlds on your planet, as well as the other planets that your Mother Earth is in alignment with. This gateway opens the door to all tribal information through time.

The tribes that I so speak of are the beginning bloodlines on your planet. There is a great record room in this gateway or stargate. This record room has the DNA systems of the collective tribes and where and how they cross-seeded to be able to vibrate in physical matter on the Earth plane.

When this stargate opens, it will start releasing karmic vapors, or emotions, which are stored in the collective bloodline of the tribes. This will start freeing and healing the separation between Souls, or Cells.

The stargate in Peru may be one of the last to open. It will open as the tribes of you come together as one.

If it opened before the other gateways, it would blow the chakra system of your planet out. The heart and mind must be in alignment, in agreement, and in harmony for the energy of the root to open.

You could say this stargate is the kundalini of your planet. You may have heard of people's kundalinis opening up before the rest of their chakras were opened. Sometimes, this creates a major blowout of their electrical system, which takes years to heal. This would also be true for your planet. Remember, you are a collective consciousness. You have many Beings who are star seeds that are on Mother Earth that have great vibrational sound frequencies. They align with other star Beings collectively and are able to do great work individually and collectively to heal the Shadow on the Earth.

### Stargate in Japan

Another stargate is under Mt. Fuji in Japan. Mt. Fuji has a very large crystal city placed above it. This crystal city threads its energy through the mountain and into the crystal stargate under the mountain. This stargate is a master activator for all of the crystal cities that have been placed above your cities around your world. As you move through the 2012 Portal, there is a coding that will be activated, and it will download, or activate, the stargate, which will download the crystalline structures into the Souls and bodies of the cities.

When the stargate opens, it will send a higher sound frequency into the crystalline structure of Mother Earth. This crystal stargate has a direct link through the meridian system throughout your universe to the Central Sun. Your Earth is moving into the Golden Ray of My consciousness, which is the Christ Ray that is generated by the Central Sun's energy.

It is not just you in human form who are the Second Coming of Christ. Mother Earth is also the Second Coming. There is no separation between you and the Soul of your Earth. You are doing this Ascension together.

As you go through the 2012 Portal, this stargate will open and allow the golden nectar of you, the Christ energy, to permeate the grids and Soul of your planet. At the same time that this stargate opens to the flow of the Golden Ray, a spiritual stargate in the heavens will open, and the Earth will glide into freedom. When this happens, the Souls that are you now inhabiting the Earth will also have their etheric bodies' vibration turned up, and you and the Christ Golden Ray frequency will come together as one. You will have moved into the center of the Golden Age.

There are many stargates that are strategically placed throughout your world. They are all connected to a stargate grid system, which is monitored by My master computer system and generated by the Central Sun's energy.

### Mount Shasta Open and Active Live Stargate

Mount Shasta has a great Stargate, which is very active and open today. There are many other stargates such as this one, but this is the largest and most active. It is a gateway for a collective extraterrestrial civilization that lives under the mountain.

The Beings in this high civilization are star seeds that come from many worlds and are constantly monitoring, protecting, and realigning the grid system and matrix of your world. This world, your holographic Earth, is the core base for all civilizations to come together as one.

As I said, you have many different E.T. races, which have reincarnated on the Earth plane to assist in the karmic completion of the end times. Great ascended Masters, Archangels, Commanders, Priestesses, and many other awakened Beings from all planets and dimensions are living together in harmony in this base. Through this active stargate, they are able to travel in and out of time simultaneously. They hold the light, or sound frequency, and consciousness from their star systems energy for the Earth. This is very much needed because many of you E.T.'s now living on Earth need the vibration from your own planetary system to sustain your life force.

This is how many of you on the Earth are able to stay balanced enough to stay connected to your light bodies. These Beings monitoring and protecting your Earth are aspects of you. They are assisting to hold your vibration through the grid system of Mother Earth. This grounds you through compatible frequencies to assist you to want to stay on Earth.

Because the Earth is a hologram of endings and new beginnings and is continuing to turn on its axis, it is emitting a color-sound frequency of death and rebirth. This creates a combustion of light that disintegrates the frequency of the collective karmic structure.

The E.T. civilization in Mt. Shasta constantly monitors and balances the meridian system of the Earth, and because you are the Cells of the planet, you also receive a frequency adjustment in your etheric DNA systems. This activates the memories in your physical DNA of a death and rebirth. This is what you and your planet are going through now.

This is how the doorways, the 11-11 and 12-12, 20-12, 13-13 and all other passageways are opening. You collectively are creating a combustion of light, which moves you out of form and into a higher collective Knowingness. Every time this happens, you and your whole world receive a higher instruction, or intention, which awakens you in the collective.

Mount Shasta is the greatest, largest, live, activated and open portal and stargate. It is holding the light for you and the Earth in this agreement of Ascension and enlightenment. Many other activated and open stargates are vibrating together with this major gateway. They are also assisting all of the E.T. races on your planet to be able to hold their frequency.

As you continue to move beyond time and through the portals opening up for you, you will find yourself merging together through these stargate portals. There will be no separation between your vibration-sound frequency and your brothers and sisters of light who maintain these stargates. You will remember that you are them, and they are you.

# HEALING THE SEPARATION BETWEEN THE MALE AND FEMALE

# LUCIA

*"Your heart will be your way of perceiving life."*

This is Lucia, Goddess of Light. I come to you today to assist you to reclaim your feminine. Your feminine is being restored to you along with your feminine power. You have been rewoven with Us, so that as the collective feminine, We will now hold the light, strength, and power for you to rethread through the feminine, back to the highest feminine of Sophia. You are great spiritual warriors; you are now opening the door for the feminine in all dimensions to rethread with, and through, you. This restoration will assist the feminine in both the female and male to reconnect to the Mother Sophia. We love you and honor you. We are with you now and always and are eternally grateful for your willingness to become one with the Sisterhood of light and to lead all back into the balance of Oneness.

*Your Sisterhood of Light*

# SOPHIA

I am with you now My children. Your journey has been long and hard, and the end is very near, not the end of your physical lives, but the end of your karmic imbalance between the male and female, between the light and Shadow.

Now is the time for the male and female to face one another, and move through the veils fearlessly, back to the core of their Beingness, their heart. My feminine awakened the Creator's, your Father's, heart. It was difficult for Him at first because He had feelings and emotions of the great pain and sorrow of the collective separation between the male and female of His creation. You beautiful children are now playing out and moving through these last stages of separation. You are now returning to Us, integrating Our heart and mind.

You are awakening and remembering that you are the master within yourself, that you are Us, that you are the Co-Creators of your purpose, your life, your joy, happiness and destiny. You are remembering that We have agreed together to assist this beautiful planet and all of its inhabitants and consciousnesses into Ascension and enlightenment.

You are in the greatest awakening that your Soul collectively has ever experienced. We are coming home together – in love, peace, and grace.

When the feminine heart started awakening in both the male and female, it created much conflict.

There became what is perceived to be a power struggle between the male and female. This is the unthreading that is happening on your planet today. In reality, what was happening was both aspects of the male and female started experiencing themselves. As they started feeling themselves, they started vibrating in a higher vibration with each other. They were truly feeling each other for the first time. As they mirrored themselves back to one another, the male experienced the magnificent presence of the feminine. This is the awakening of the heart of both the male and female throughout all Creations now.

You are going to have many opportunities to love and balance your male and female within between now and the 2012 Portal and beyond into the 13-13 portal within yourself. You will have the opportunity to choose another consciousness, or way of living. You, the light ones, will find that as you are merging more and more into your Shadow, your light will transmute this old energy into Self-Realization. Your whole perspective and perception on life will continue to shift, and old beliefs and paradigms will fall to the wayside, releasing old veils of illusion. Your heart will be your way of perceiving life.

From this experience, you will find the truth of who you are and what your real purpose and mission is. Your vibrations will become higher, and all you will see in one another is each other's love and divinity. You will see this because that is what you will experience yourself as.

You are emerging collectively out of the cocoon of the caterpillar and into the freedom of the butterfly. In this frequency, you will feel yourself as the crystal consciousness of Me, the heart of Creation.

You will experience the lightness of your Being higher than you have ever imagined it to be. You are an emerging love-light frequency of total consciousness of the heart of Me. You are remembering who you are and rethreading collectively with each other's love and light and are shifting the whole consciousness of your planet into Ascension and enlightenment.

It is most important that you hold love and light for all on your planet to reawaken and remember who they are.

# THE 60'S FLOWER CHILDREN – THE FEMININE HEART OPENING FOR THE EARTH

*"Those of you who have vibrated together in this great heart awakening opened the doorway for all to be able to merge back together in love, free will, and choice."*

Your Flower Children, the children of the sixties, opened the doorway of the heart. Many of you are these children, the Indigos, who reincarnated collectively with this as your mission: to move the collective into a higher vibration by opening the heart and expanding the mind's conception of love.

Many of you have now recycled, reincarnated, back to assist the Earth in opening her heart to move through all gateways and into the 13-13 within yourself. You will continue to open many portals of light shifting the consciousness into a new lifetime on the Earth without physically leaving the body. You have agreed to be the Co-Creators with Me of Heaven on Earth. We are coming full circle, back into the true Garden of Eden, where the male and female mirror and honor each other's love-light and magnificence.

You are awakening into My heart with My beloved Sophia

and into the breath and flow of love, of Our Creation. You are now vibrating in the highest consciousness of your Soul/Cell agreements and are in alignment with the Mother Earth's heart assisting her to return home to her beloved Father Earth.

These alignments have a beautiful color sound frequency that opens portals of light assisting Mother Earth and yourselves to ascend.

In the 20th century, many doorways opened. Look at the evolution of the Souls/Cells of your planet that took place in a 100-year cycle. Look at how quickly walls and barriers broke down and fell apart. The sixties were a major heart opening agreement. Those of you who vibrated together in this heart awakening opened the doorway for all to be able to merge back together in love, free will, and choice and your collective Souls' Song and music.

Many doorways are continuing to open, and all is being exposed so that you collectively can open a new passageway through the heart into Ascension, enlightenment, and into a rebirth of love.

# RIDING THE LIGHT-LOVE RAYS
# TO FREEDOM

*"When you are in the color-sound vibration of your collective Soul, you will find laughter and joy in all of your experiences."*

Your Souls' agreement is to now move beyond fear-based duality.

Take your power back from drugs, alcohol, conditioned love, and the confusion between love and sex, addictions, food, fear, and so on. All of these addictions are fear-based: fear of your own power, fear of your feelings of your magnificence, fear of your own love, fear of success and fear of your grand purpose on the Earth plane.

I speak to you of these programs so that you will become aware of them and will know where to go to release and heal them. Everything you are doing and have done in this lifetime is by agreement. You are not victims, unless you allow yourselves to be. You have chosen to go through these experiences so that you will know where you need to go to heal, to love yourselves, so that you can love and live fully in the now.

You have chosen these lessons to free your Soul. There are two sides to every coin. Instead of looking at the negative, say to yourself, "Thank you God/Creator. Thank you for showing me this lesson, so I can release my attachment to it." You may not understand the lesson at the time or even know why you are going through it, but if you give thanks for the lesson, you are disempowering the negative.

When you give thanks, you are aligning your God-I AM, with the I AM of Creation. You are saying, "I am now willing to understand what I have agreed to go through to free my Soul." As you continue to give thanks and ask to understand the lesson, your I AM will shine the light so brightly that you will become crystal clear and will learn from and release the lesson.

The more you do this, the more you move out of the victim role. Believe it or not, you are not victims; you are volunteers. Maybe you didn't understand the lesson in another lifetime, and you came back again to not only understand it, but also to heal, release, embrace, and retrieve your light from the pattern.

Everything is by agreement. If you have agreed to go through these lessons, you can now agree to release them. You do this through intention by the "power of the spoken word." You would say out loud:

*"I release the karmic collective consciousness of all reversed programming; all programming that reverses my love, light, magnificence, and purpose to karmic fear, and of all lifetimes when I was afraid of my power. I am Love and Light. I trust and believe the consciousness has changed. I am now safe in Love and Light. I AM. I AM. I AM."*

You are powerful Beings, Souls and Cells of My and your Father's highest consciousness. Rethread with Us. See your cup full instead of empty. Soon your cup will be so full of love and the magnificence of life that it will spill over. You will have so much magic to share with others.

You are now coming into a new lifetime without physically leaving the body, and it is most important to build a new foundation. That new foundation is your Father and I, as your real parents – your Souls'/Cells' origin. As you stay connected to Us, We will continually assist you to access higher vibrations of yourselves. You will open up and reactivate your Creator DNA.

As you continue to turn your vibration up, eventually you will move beyond duality and the Shadow, individually and collectively. Nothing will be able to penetrate you that is not love and light. Your DNA vibration will be One with Ours.

You will always have a Shadow, but you will have unthreaded from the fear Ego consciousness. This self-awakened Shadow will support your light self in the highest. As long as you continue to vibrate in the highest consciousness and integrity, you and your Shadow will continue to vibrate together in harmony.

See all in your life as a gift. When you are truly willing to do this, you will start your journey home within yourself very quickly. If you see all as a gift, you are aligning your thought frequencies and patterns with the highest vibration of Creation. You have set the intention to move out of duality.

Because you are now Co-Creators of your experience and what some may call destiny, you have the power to re-arrange your energy thought patterns by your intention, or conscious agreements. If you think negative fear thoughts, you will bring more negative fear energies and experiences back to you. If you think and see all of your life's experiences as great teachers to expand your thinking and consciousness, you will bring great life-expanding, healing experiences back to you. You will bring other Soul travelers with the same desire and frequency back to you. As you do this, and plug into each other's energy, or mirror each other's energy, the light will be so bright that you will feel yourself in a constant natural high. This high will be beyond any experience that any mind-altering substance could ever give you.

You will be connecting your own Soul's song and light frequency to your collective Souls' songs and frequencies. You will ride on the waves of love and light with one another, lifting each other into a higher memory of your magnificence.

As you ride the light-love waves collectively, you will never, ever feel alone again.

As you are back together in your Soul Group's song, you will be able to laugh at your own process. There will be no need to take yourself so seriously. As you continue to raise your vibration through the Ascension process, you will be unable to take yourself or your journey so seriously. As you are connected to yourself, of Us, in a higher frequency, there is no judgment. There is only honor for you and your willingness to be on the Earth plane at this time.

Thank you for everything that you agreed to go through to heal yourself and the collective. Forgive yourself for all of your beliefs and perceptions. Love yourself for the great Being of light that you are. Then love yourself some more.

# HEALING THE FEMININE THROUGH SELF-LOVE

*"Love is the language that continues to grow and expand all consciousness."*

Judgment towards self and others comes from a lower karmic frequency. As you connect to higher understanding, you will experience that there is only love for you and your willingness to assist the evolution of consciousness.

Because We are one, you will feel this great love and appreciation for yourself. How could We not love you when you were created by Us? You are Us.

The more you move into Our love of you and for you, the more you experience self-love. The more you experience self-love, the easier it is for your planet's Ascension and enlightenment. When you move into the place of self-love, you see all as love, even what in the past you may have judged, or condemned. All is love and in its perfection.

As you see and experience all as love, the karmic fear frequency starts breaking up and dissipating. Love is the highest vibration and essence. There is no energy field that can come up against it or hold any vibration against it.

The power of love can lift and move mountains: mountains being karmic turbulence. Nothing that is fear-based can continue to exist in love. The love essence, or frequency, will break loose and dissipate all fear-based illusions.

Love will set you free and allow you to come home again inside of yourself. Love is. Love is your Creation, your salvation, your freedom. Love is your agreement in this lifetime.

I hear Souls ask, "What is my purpose in this lifetime?" As the veils of illusion are dissipating, many of you know and feel that you are on the Earth for a reason. I hear you say and ask yourselves, others, and Us, "What is my purpose? What is my mission? I can feel that I am on the Earth for a reason. What is it?"

I say to you, your whole purpose on the Earth at this time is to experience unconditional self-love. Love is it. Whatever the question, love is the answer.

When you move into the vibration and consciousness of love, that is all you will see; that is all you will experience. You will constantly mirror back to others their love and magnificence.

When this love mirror vibrates into a fellow Soul traveler, their old guards and walls start breaking up and dissipating. They start remembering who they are. Old prejudices, hatreds, belief systems, and fears start losing their power. As the structure of the old dis-ease breaks loose, it starts unraveling from the collective pattern. The collective fear-based pattern loses its grip. This has a domino effect. As the Cell/Soul breaks loose from the collective pattern, this newfound expression of self-love sends the power of love energy into the collective pattern.

As you love yourselves, you break a link in the fear pattern. From this broken chain, or missing link, the collective frequency of love can be downloaded into the pattern.

This is your Souls' agreement in this lifetime: to love yourself beyond duality. As you achieve this, you align your frequency with other aspects of yourself in other dimensions that are already vibrating beyond duality.

You are the Cells of the collective moving into a higher frequency; you are aligning with higher frequencies in all dimensions. All consciousness is continuing to evolve. As above, so below. All is connected. Nothing is separate from one another. All Souls and Cells are one. This is you ascending, re-connecting to yourself collectively, moving into one consciousness of love – of all knowing of the I AM of All That Is.

All beliefs, or perceptions, of separation have been illusions. You have been in a dream, or for some of you, it could feel as if the dream was a nightmare from which you could not seem to awaken. You are now awakening from this illusional dream. The veils are being lifted, or dissipated, and you are experiencing all aspects of yourself in all dimensions. You have coding patterns in your DNA that are now being activated, expanding you into your multi-dimensional selves. You are vibrating with, and turning the light on all aspects of yourselves that have been in fear or conflict. Everywhere you turn, you are seeing yourself, for all is you.

You could not see other Cells'/Souls' magnificence if you did not have the memory of your own light or magnificence. You would not feel anger, fear, prejudice, hate, and so on, if you did not have the experience or energy frequency inside of you.

All is you and mirroring you back to you. As you love all aspects of yourself that you see, or experience, in your own mirror, or reflection, you move out of what you could call the Ugly Duckling stage of not belonging, fitting in, or knowing who you are.

You become the beautiful swan that fits in everywhere and

vibrates together with all in love. You become the geese that fly together on the wings and energy of one another. Sometimes, with your formation, you are the leader. At other times, you may shift to the back or side and hold the frequency for another to lead, to shine, and to be supported in their strength and magnificence.

At this time, you become comfortable in your own skin, just for being you. You accept yourself for all that you are and all that you think you are not. This is self-love. You no longer feel the need to show others your self-importance, or value, because you feel such a balance of love and acceptance within yourself. This is the true awakening and healing of the feminine, through self-love.

# WALKING HUMBLY

*"As you look at all of your enlightened Masters and teachers on your planet, they all have unique gifts, or jewels, to assist others with, and yet, none have the whole basket of jewels. You are now awakening into the Masters and Co-Creators within yourself, and your unique gifts are being remembered."*

It is most important on one's Soul journey that you walk humbly. As you walk humbly, you are connecting to the highest heart mind of All That Is. When you walk humbly, you have moved to the place in your Soul's evolution where you have nothing to prove. You do not have to show anyone how much you know, what you have done, or where you have been.

Your greatest purpose in this lifetime is to love yourself enough so that you can move in and out of all consciousness and dimensions.

There may be a time when you will be asked for your input, insights, or understanding. There may be other times when you will be asked to support another Soul/Cell of you as they speak, or share, their knowledge and Knowingness with others.

This is truly knowing that all of you on the Earth have come together with a piece of a great puzzle. As you love and accept yourself enough, you will open your heart and mind to your fellow travelers to find their way home to you. This fellow traveler has a piece of the puzzle that seems to fit next to yours. The piece of the puzzle is truly a vibration of the consciousness, which is being downloaded to you on the

Earth at this time; it is being awakened and activated in your DNA. You are to come together, each of you, with a piece of the higher consciousness, or Knowingness, of Creation.

As you are now the co-creators of this mission to bring the higher understanding to the Earth, you are to bring all pieces together to create the whole puzzle, or what seems to be a puzzle. Those of you who have chosen to be the gatekeepers to this higher wisdom are now opening the doorways, or gateways, for the puzzles of Creation: who you are, where you came from, who is God, what is God? Is there life on other planets? These questions are coming to the forefront. As you, the gatekeepers, open the doorways for your piece of the puzzle to be opened and remembered, you are doing so for the whole collective of you.

Each piece of the puzzle, or gateway, has its own vibrations of color and sound frequency. As the gateway opens, it allows the information from all dimensions of like frequency to come through it and connect to all of the Souls on Earth, to re-awaken and align with the frequency of self in all other dimensions.

The Earth is healing and awakening as your DNA is rethreading back together, cleaning out the veils of illusion, and realigning you in total Knowingness. As one Cell/Soul attains this state of attunement, it mirrors this frequency back to many, so they can also move through duality and back to the highest vibrations of I AM.

Each gateway, or puzzle piece, vibrates through all Creation. When you bring all pieces back together, or all gateways are open, you have the whole puzzle, or all channels, of Creation open. With all channels open, you will continually readjust the frequencies and move into higher aspects of yourself through all dimensions and Creations. As you do this, you are vibrating beyond a time frequency where thought creates all. It is at that moment that you are truly the co-creators of your own life, world, and destiny.

What does walking humbly have to do with this? Your purpose is to love yourself enough to know that you are all you have ever looked for or wanted. Your entire search for truth is within you.

This is great power. From humility, you no longer have anything to prove to yourself. Whenever you feel you have to let others see how much you know, you are still trying to prove to yourself that you are important, or valuable.

Once you know your importance and value through self-love, you can move into humility, or humbleness. From this place, you are in total honor of all around you. You are in honor of the power of Creation. You are in honor of the Souls of your brothers and sisters for their agreements to be on the Earth and for everything they have agreed to go through and are going through.

In humility, you experience all in love, or full bloom. You see all in the birth process of Creation. When you walk humbly, you walk, talk, feel, and communicate from the heart's frequency of love. From this love, you are able to be great teachers of strength and knowing just by your being. You become the pillars of love and strength to mirror back to all their love and magnificence.

You become and hold the highest I AM frequency with other great Masters and teachers in all dimensions. You vibrate beyond karmic time. Your eyes, the windows of your Soul, are in constant love and gratitude for All That Is.

You will give thanks for All That Is and for all around you. You will feel secure enough to vibrate in the background, if that is what is needed. Your energy will be in total alignment with Creation. Your life will be in a constant flow. Your needs and wants will always be met because you will be vibrating in total Creation energy.

You will find your desires will become much simpler, and yet, all of your life's experience much fuller. You will be constantly aware of yourself as others. You will feel no separation. Your greatest desire will be to commune with God, Creator all the time. Nature will become a greater experience of Creation for you. Your physical vision will open up, and you will see colors very alive and vibrant.

In your Bible, it is written that the meek shall inherit the world. The meek are not those who are frightened, or shy. The meek are those who walk humbly among you and have the greatest connection with Source. They inherit the world's highest vibration, or consciousness. They become co-creators of your world's highest intent. They realign with their innocence and inheritance of love and light, of All That Is.

To be the gatekeepers, you must move into a place of humility to be able to serve in the highest. You must walk humbly among your peers. You must always have their and your best interests in your heart. You must see all as you. It is then that you will assist to open the Pearly Gates of what you on your planet call Heaven.

You will be the gatekeepers who have moved beyond Ego, beyond fear. You will hold your gate open at the precise moment that it is needed and bring your piece of the puzzle, or consciousness, back with the collective to assist the whole planet and its Cells of you into enlightenment. **And so it is.**

# COMPLETING KARMICALLY

You have 12 primary lifetimes and then many lives that extend from the primary. I speak to you of lifetimes because you are in a time frame. You actually have 12 lifetimes going on simultaneously. You may even be living more than one lifetime on the Earth at the same time. You may be living lifetimes on other planets, and even universes, or perhaps, as a Spirit guide or Master, guiding you and others in this lifetime.

Each primary lifetime has its own karmic wheel and has a higher self-consciousness guiding it. Each wheel has a primary astrological sign, which is the center, or core, of the wheels, and the spokes of the wheel are all 12 signs of the Zodiac.

Each wheel's higher self vibrates in the highest consciousness of your OverSoul.

You begin each life with a Divine Blueprint, which is your astrological sign. This sign energetically sets up your personality and the way you will experience life. This is the lens of perception that you will see through, to learn the lessons you need, to feed the information back to your Master Soul.

Many of you on the Earth plane are the light warriors who are in the last stages of your karmic wheels. You have experienced many perceptions, or lifetimes, through the blueprints, or astrological signs, and are now here to move beyond all wheels and back together with your OverSoul. Your agreement is to now integrate with your higher self – to move beyond karmic time to re-create a new lifetime on the Earth Plane as the Master and Co-Creator, vibrating in our Souls' highest collective knowing.

Your whole Soul's journey has been with your own design. If you have had a difficult learning schedule in a lifetime, you may choose a few lifetimes in between to balance out in love, light, joy, and happiness before re-entering another heavier journey. This would be like you on the Earth plane going to school and wanting to complete quickly. You may take many difficult classes, and in doing so, not have much time for yourself to play or have fun. When you finish school, you may decide to take a year or so off before going into the next step of your journey.

Your Soul's journey is the school. You may feel that your last school load was quite difficult and take time off before going back to the next phase of what you have studied or learned. If you did not take time off to relax, rest, and have fun in between lifetimes on your Soul's journey into and beyond duality, it would be too difficult. You would not have the balance to see what you have experienced, or learned. You would become so immersed in your emotional experience that you would lose the connection to your higher aspect of self, which is your guiding light.

You see this is happening much on your planet now. Because there is so much duality going on and being projected to you and your planet from the media and other forms, many of you are immersing yourself in the negativity and forgetting to balance yourself out.

It is most important because the more balanced you become, the more you can remember your own light and magnificence. As you do this, you will connect with the collective light of the I AM and download it to your planet to break up the collective fear Shadow.

You must stay balanced to be able to connect with the other collective light Beings. You are the Second Coming of Christ, the Golden Ray, and must take time out daily to meditate and be able to stay connected to your Christ light collectively. Eventually, your Golden Christ Light will permeate all Beings who forgot who they were.

Because you are in a holographic universe and experience your life from all color-light frequencies, depending on where your Souls/Cells are vibrating at the moment, you now also have the choice to choose what ending you want. You are the collective ending to the illusion play of "duality." Your intention, or agreement, is to come together collectively in your Soul Group's songs, expand yourself into another Soul Group's song and then into another, so all songs support each other to turn on the light and thread back into the divine matrix, to lift the whole consciousness on your planet back into the light.

This sound vibration can be heard throughout your planet, as you are literally calling yourselves back to one another. This is where your free will steps in. You are vibrating collectively in the light and are still carrying memories of karmic lifetimes in your Cells, which create a Shadow over your own light.

The way to break this karmic fear cycle is to set your intention to be in the highest vibration of your own light. As you set this as your intention, your 'inner' net system will draw to you other Souls of light consciousness with the same intention of awakening.

Like attracts like. All in life mirrors you through all dimensions. When you ask through prayer, your emotional body's vibration becomes so high that Beings of light in all dimensions feel the call, or frequency, of the call, and start downloading their light into you.

Your intention to heal, to love yourself, to love others, and to assist the Earth Mother into Ascension is your Soul's agreement!

As you move through the illusions and life seems to become too difficult, your gift to yourself is that you can start setting intention for your life to become easier. When this call is heard and answered, many Souls/Cells may temporarily feel that life becomes even more difficult. This is because the light hits the Cells and starts waking up all of the illusional aspects of you. You might feel like you could end up losing everything. You are actually awakening and letting go of the illusions of who you thought you were, or what you thought was important to you. You can see that this is happening collectively on your planet now.

As you continue to let go of the old illusions, you will start bringing into your life beautiful mirrors of yourself, of your own light. You then start feeling glimmers of hope that maybe there is a way out. What was so important to you in the past may no longer matter.

When this happens, the Ego mind within you becomes frightened and sends the message out to the collective Ego mind. You may feel yourself having a difficult time being or staying centered because the Ego Shadow tries to pull you back into old emotions by activating fears, beliefs, and addictions.

Do not go to battle with your Shadow or the collective Shadow unless it is your Soul's agreement to be a slayer of the dragons. It is most important that you now become the peaceful warrior. If you fight against your Ego Shadow, you empower it. You are now moving out of the Spiritual Warrior consciousness and into the Peacemaker. All doors are now open for you. Collectively set the intention to move towards peace and it shall be!

Thank the Shadow for being such a great teacher. Thank it for holding the mirror for you to see and experience what needs to be loved and healed within you. Continue to love your Shadow.

As the light and love dissipate the Ego Shadow's hold on you, it will start retreating and releasing old illusions. The only place you can be is here now. If you continue to vibrate in past memories, you bring the past into the now of you and thread it into what is called the future of you.

Sometimes, it is most difficult to be in the now because your emotional body is still vibrating in belief systems, or structures, that thread through all karmic wheels. This sound vibration can be heard throughout your planet, as you are literally calling yourselves back to one another.

Sometimes this creates mixed feelings in your bodies, which creates an imbalance. Perhaps, your bodies carry a memory of being harmed or hurt when your intention in the past was to awaken spiritually. If this is the case, your body will turn on the memory of the hurt, and it may re-manifest itself in the physical through the emotions of the experience creating sickness or dis-ease. See this as a gift, or opportunity, to be able to release it.

The illness, or dis-ease, always has a frame of reference elsewhere; as this is the lifetime you have agreed to come full circle. When the sickness, or dis-ease, remanifests itself, it is because it is asking you to love it and embrace it as a great teacher so that you can let it go. It is emerging again so that you can release it through love.

When you can find the frame of reference from the pattern, you can usually release the dis-ease. All that awakens within you in this lifetime is here to be loved and embraced. The more you go through the veils, the easier it is to be in the now.

Soon your subconscious will be used to sending love and light into the pattern and will immediately go into action. You must continue to support your subconscious in the positive. As your subconscious opens the door for the light and love to download into the emotion, it will instantly release. You will no longer have to find the frame of reference. Your bodies will know all consciousness is in the now.

This is easy to do by using a mantra that will change the frequency of the negative thought. The mantra could even be the word love.

From this, you will have such a strong core foundation of the highest I AM and light that nothing that is not light will be able to penetrate your core. Everything that happens to you will strengthen your core because your subconscious will send the memory to all of your bodies' minds of love, light, health, and wholeness.

You have agreed to come to the Earth and move through all 12 parallel lifetimes and blend them together as one.

Because you are each other, when you blend together with all aspects of yourself in all Matrices and move beyond your karmic wheels, you will pull many with you because they are you; they are Me.

If you were not continuing to move through your Souls'

wheels and turning on your karmic axis, you would not have available to you all of the magnificence aspects of yourself mirroring you back into love and forgiveness.

Because you are all the Cells of the karmic wheel, this self-love vibration sends the beautiful love sound through all Creations of the Divine Matrix.

It is then, that you will merge together beyond any time frame and into the highest agreement of your Soul. You will have awakened into the Master of Creation and become a Spiritual Teacher, a guiding confidante, etc., in whatever way, or realm, in which you choose to serve.

# HEALING TWIN FLAME SEPARATION

*"In the higher consciousness of your Being, your*
*healthy, accepted, and well-adjusted male is loving and*
*supporting your loving and caring, sensitive feminine."*

You are now co-creating Heaven on Earth. You have agreed to awaken into the memory of Me to hold the vibration of enlightenment for all. When you are out of body form and home in the highest, you are with your Twin Flames and partners. To be the highest Co-Creator of Me on Earth, it is important that you are in physical form vibrating with the highest balance of your male and female within.

Now on the Earth, many of you are bringing back to you relationships that are soulmate intended and mistaking them for Twin Flame partnerships. Soulmate relationships are Souls/Cells with whom you have had many relationships and lifetimes. You know each other so well, and when you reconnect with one another, you experience the joy of reunion, of family coming back together.

Many of you on the Earth are not from the Earth, meaning it is not your planet of origin. You are the end time players who have come to the Earth to assist the whole consciousness into Ascension. Your vibration is different and even more sensitive than others' vibration on the Earth. You feel as though you do not fit or belong. You have felt separate for a long time and have had such a longing to go back home.

You then meet a Soul who feels the same way, and you have a kindred relationship. You bond with each other in the separateness, which you have felt for so long. You are like plugs, or extension cords, from other frequencies and are looking for someplace to plug into, to feel connected.

Because you have felt so separate, you feel very connected with each other in your not belonging. At first, you feel at home: this is my partner. Finally, I have my divine relationship. Then your separateness, which has not been healed, mirrors itself to one another. All of your hurt, abandonment, fear of love and intimacy, and all of your frozen emotions start mirroring back to one another.

When it becomes too difficult, the relationship dissolves, and you start looking for someplace else to plug yourself into so that you will feel wanted, important, and valuable. Because you are vibrating in that beginning memory vibration of the collective separation, you bring constant mirrors of this loneliness and separation back to you. You do this so that you can start healing the split.

You bring the same relationship with a different face back to you time and time again until you realize this relationship is not separate from you. It is you. You are looking at yourself in the mirror, to have reflected back to you, yourself.

The more you can love this reflection of yourself who is you, you will start shattering the walls, or veils, of illusion and separation. If you allow yourself to truly know that what you see is you, what you dislike is you, what you hate is you, and what you love and admire is you, you will then be able to heal and love yourself.

Every thing or person who mirrors you is a gift of love that you have asked to come to you, to free your Soul from lifetimes of separation.

Many times, your true partner, or Twin Flame, could come up in front of you, and you would not recognize him or her because who you think you are supposed to be with comes from your perception of who or what you think love is.

The more you allow yourself to love you by looking at all mirror aspects of you and releasing these fear patterns, the more you can accept yourself for your totality. The loneliness and separateness that you have felt so much in your life starts to dissipate. As you love yourself unconditionally, you can start loving others unconditionally. You cannot truly see another for their love and magnificence until you love yourself. All is a mirror of you, and all you bring to you is you. Their love and magnificence is your own love and magnificence.

As you continue to expand into your own self-love, you will bring a partnership into your life who can and wants to love you. You will no longer draw to yourself your own separateness and loneliness. You will draw to you, your love, innocence, and magnificence.

As you release the veils of separateness and start loving yourself, you begin to balance the male and female aspects of self. Your heart starts loving all of you, including your own male (mind-Ego-will) self. You will see what you used to believe were your shortcomings are now your gifts. These gifts of a strong will were your survival techniques. Your strong will gave you the strength to bring you back to the place where you could recognize yourself as love.

Because all is you, your purest intention can start unraveling your world from fear, break the karmic sound barrier, and penetrate the collective karmic structure sending waves of light and love and rethreading the structure into its highest form. When you reach this state of enlightenment, your Soul's agreement is to expand this consciousness to others.

When you have direct communication, or contact, with the total balance of Me and your Mother Sophia, you start releasing old fears and start shedding old beliefs and misperceptions within yourself. A vibrational flame of love connects to the memory within you of harmony and balance before you separated, or split, from your divine partner into a karmic time frame.

As you feel Our vibration of love, this love and light penetrates the cell structure and re-activates the safety of love and your divine partnership within you. This has a sound effect, which harmonizes through all of your bodies, balancing them in love-light consciousness. Most of your body is fluid, and when this complete balanced love of the male and female vibrates through your body, a great healing takes place.

You feel your bodies open up. Sometimes, you want to cry because the love is so strong that it starts cleaning out your fears and misperceptions of love. You may sometimes feel tears and emotions when you hear a beautiful song that touches your heart and Soul. The frequency of the song resonates with your frequency and starts breaking loose frozen emotions connected to what you perceive, or experience, as the pain, hurt, loneliness, abandonment, and so on, connected to the original split of your Soul.

Look at all the music in your world. Not all music resonates with everybody. One of you may hear a song that touches your Soul deeply, while it may not affect the person next to you at all. This is because you are all beautiful notes of Me. You are not all the same note, yet as you, the Cells of Me, connect with your one note, or sound, in the highest, you feel fulfilled and expand yourself beyond time and perceptions. When this happens, you blend your note, sounds and song into another Cell's/Soul's song.

Soon you have a beautiful symphony of all sounds and songs blending together in perfect harmony within yourself. This perfect harmony blends you together as one and lifts your vibrations into a higher essence. The male and female coming back together in honor and joy is a beautiful song. This song will awaken and heal your world.

As Co-Creator with me, I would strongly suggest that if love of partnership is your greatest desire that you put that request on the top of the list and it shall be.

Love all aspects of yourself. Bring your male and female inner children together so they can love and support each other. Allow your heart to assist to quiet your mind. Love your Ego and Shadow into self-realization. Love all aspects of yourself; all that you are and all that you think you aren't. Love yourself, love yourself, and love yourself some more. Remember, like attracts like.

Together We will create love for you because love is who you are. It is your birthright to now have love. I will support you in your greatest desire because I am you and love is my greatest intention of all. Your request for this divine love aligns with My request of you. Love is Our purpose, Our quest, and your divine birthright.

Self-love needs to awaken within you so that when you come together in divinity with your own divine partnership and Flame, you have already moved much of the old unconsciousness out of the way. You can recognize each other, take the hand of one another in sacredness, and lead each other as one. As We become one in the balance of the male and female, you hold this energy field for other flames to reconnect, or find, each other.

This is your greatest show on Earth, the time that you have waited for since the illusion of separation. You are coming home with all consciousness.

# OPENING HEAVEN'S DOOR – THROUGH THE HEART

*"You are love. You were created in love. It is now your agreement and birthright to awaken to your own self-love and acceptance and to collectively align yourselves with love of all others that are you."*

You are moving into a frequency of enlightenment. Enlightenment means to lighten up. The energy of your planet is becoming very high as Mother Earth is giving birth to a new wave of consciousness. You, the Cells and inhabitants of her, are the new wave, or frequency, of thinking, of feeling.

There is much talk of enlightenment, and Beings are now setting their intent to be light and to have fun, joy, and love. Many on your planet have already moved into the beginning stages of enlightenment. This is because you have already moved through many of the karmic paradigms and wheels and are back into the center of your Souls' journey, which is the center of your heart.

The only way you can move into the kingdom of Heaven is through your heart. You need not wait until your Soul leaves your body, or vehicle. You can reach that state within your heart. This is enlightenment. When you move into a place of love for all Souls, both light and Shadow and any variations in between and experience all that you see beyond any story, you move into the place of enlightenment. When you see all as you and can love all as you, you have moved beyond duality and into Beingness, into the Isness. When you arrive at this place, you are beyond karma and vibrating in the higher consciousness.

As you start moving into enlightenment, your judgments towards one another, the world, and the Shadow start disappearing. You no longer feel the need to feed the negative or to speak unkindly to one another. You feel like you can no longer listen to fear-based theories, programs, or beliefs. You no longer wish to participate in the negative. You start seeing more of the beauty of life. You experience all as a rebirth of consciousness. Everywhere you turn, you start seeing and experiencing the light and good in one another.

Your sensitivity to nature and one another will heighten. You will find yourself more in love with yourself and others. You will be consciously aware of old judgments and will experience yourself witnessing the judgments, or Ego mind, and not reacting. You will truly be the witness of all of your life. Being in the moment will be very important to you, because you will know and feel that the past was an illusion, an old story.

As you move through the veils and experience the now of you, you will experience all aspects of life through your own magnificence, seeing all as you. There will be no sense of separation between you and others. Being in your body will feel comfortable and joyful. You will feel excited about being on the Earth at this time and also in your ability to assist in the great shift of consciousness into Ascension.

You and your planet are now in the Golden Age. You are in a new living frequency of a golden, light song. This frequency is penetrating your planet and all of you on your planet.

Many of you great Souls are now receiving and awakening in this frequency and choosing to change your lives by changing your perceptions. Your conscious intention is to heal the world by loving yourselves enough to be able to forgive all karmic duality.

This is your purpose: to love, love, and love some more and to love yourself enough so that you can reach out to the Souls of other travelers and love and honor them for their Soul's journey. From this love energy, you start warming the world and the Souls/Cells of the world. You may not have the means, or ability, to save Souls whose agreements were to be born into poverty, suffering, or the Shadow, but you do have the means to love them, to turn on the light within them to help them to remember who they are.

You are love. You were created in love. It is now your agreement and birthright to awaken to your own self-love and acceptance and to collectively align yourselves with the love of all others that are you. Love is such a great power that its sound frequency breaks all fear-based barriers. Love heals all wounds and allows you to come home inside of yourself.

# TAMING THE EGO – THROUGH LOVE

*"Hold your Ego. Embrace it. Love it. Disempower it."*

Your Ego does not want to surrender its power. It actually goes to war against the light consciousness part of you. If you get angry and put energy into it, you are feeding it. You give it your power. Love the Ego. Love it, and love it some more. See the Ego as a child who is throwing a tantrum because it is not receiving enough attention. The child Ego wants its own way.

When you see and recognize yourself as love, strong, and as a Being of light, your Ego will start feeling safe enough to surrender. Because the Ego is no longer in power and has been in control for so long, it will not quite know how to act or what to do in this feeling of safety.

It is important to be conscious of this. When the Ego feels threatened and feels it is being left out and wants to have a sense of power; talk to it, love it. Tell it how much you love it. Do not give it your power. Just see it as a part of you that is in a new lifetime and does not quite know what its role is … yet.

Watch the Ego. Love it and hear it, but do not surrender into it. This would be like a small child throwing a tantrum for attention. If you are angry with the child, you give the child your power. The child will continue to throw tantrums for attention. Love the child, and as you do this, the child feels acknowledged and heard.

See your Ego as your small child who may need to be heard. Observe its lack of comfort, love it, and put it to bed. Love dissipates the fear.

It is then that your Ego can unthread from the collective

Ego and become the healthy male inside of you. Your healthy, accepted, and well-adjusted male Ego can then love and support your loving and caring feminine.

Your inner male and female aspects will then love and support each other's healthy wishes and desires.

When the Ego starts throwing its tantrum, see it as two-year-old children within you who are kicking and screaming. Hold your children tight and love them. Love them. Love them. After a while, they will become exhausted and lose their power. Love is strong. Nothing can disempower love. Love is.

*See the humor in the play with the Ego. Laugh with the Ego, not at it; by doing this, you start changing the energy frequency of the patterns. Imagine magic with the Ego. Imagine the Ego at the circus. Bring unicorns, dolphins, and whales to the Ego. Talk to the Ego and thank it for being one of your greatest teachers. Tell it you no longer wish to grow and heal through duality.*

*Wrap the golden Christ blanket around your Ego, hold it, embrace it, love it, and disempower it, by placing it into the center of your golden heart. Your heart's love will soften and quiet the ego.*

Hold your ego. Embrace it. Disempower it. If you allow it to have its own way, its tantrum will become stronger and louder, and soon you will feel defeated and hopeless. You will start downloading the negative tapes of the Ego into your emotions and bring back more of the defeated patterns into your life.

Do not get into a dialogue with the Ego. Thank it. Love it.

Acknowledge it, and put it to bed. The more you do this, the more you will move into love. Do this with your individual Ego and the collective. Once again, thank it for being one of your greatest teachers. Tell it you are no longer learning through or from duality. Affirm that you are light and love. Bring your whole light team, Christ, the Masters and Angels. Ask your Highest Master team to surround you and your Ego with love and light.

Ask Jeshua and Magdalene to download Their crystal golden light into your etheric body, which holds a collective DNA system. As your etheric body fills with the golden Christ love, it will fill your whole body with love, and move you into a feeling of peace, of grace.

# ENLIGHTENMENT – YOUR TRUE SELF

*"There is only love, and as your vibration is love, that will be your experience of all existence."*

I am speaking to you of ways to move yourself into enlightenment. You are on the wave, or paradigm, of enlightenment. You must reinforce your intention with the power of your mind and hold it. As you do this, you connect with the collective intention of enlightenment (beyond karmic duality), and hold the light for one another. This is how your planet is healing, by lightening up collectively and holding the love frequency for all to feel their own self-love.

Many of you on your planet now have this understanding and are consciously aware of the ability to collectively heal the world through love.

Start your day like this:

*Set your intention to do this daily: Imagine your heart being a golden sun. Then imagine yourself in the center of this golden sun, which is the Christ energy. The more you practice this, the further you will be able to move into your heart. You will start feeling a warmth move through your body. From this warmth, you will feel a great peace.*

*When you are in the center of your golden heart, release whatever your fears, or traumas, or concerns are. Say,* **"I now release this burden (of whatever the fear is) on the Christ within and I go free."** *(The Christ love light frequency will* *dissipate the fear frequency.) This burden could be the fear of lack, of lack of prosperity, issues in relationships, depression, health, loss, traumas, guilt, shame, etc.*

*As you continue to do this daily, you will be permeating in your own love and acceptance. You will feel your own joy, love, and happiness. Remember, all in life mirrors you. As you experience yourself as love and peace, you will see and experience all as the same because all is a reflection of your inner Being. Set your intention to this daily. Bask in the pure love essence of your own heart's I AM, Christ love.*

Enlightenment, the I AM Christ, the Golden Ray of you, is now the Second Coming. You are this energy Source and have always been. You just forgot. You are moving beyond linear time and expanding into all aspects yourself. As you continue to move into the center of your Soul, you will become one with yourself in all existence. You will soon find this to be a great, rewarding time in your life. All the fruits of your efforts will ripen for you.

You will be the conscious Co-Creators of your life, having a domino effect on assisting others who are not quite conscious enough to know that they are Creator Beings. Your light, love, and highest intention will connect to the dormant aspects of their light, assisting them to awaken quickly.

As this great awakening, or quickening, takes place within you, your experience of what is important for yourself and others of your world will change. You will feel yourself as a new person. In actuality, you have shed your old veils of illusion and are remembering who you are.

Simplifying your life will also be very important to you. You will feel a great need to clear out old clutter and material things. This is most important for you to do in your process of enlightenment: lightening up, because everything is energy. Move old energy out of your life and consciousness. As you rid yourself of past material objects, you release any corded emotions connected to the past experience. You must release old energies to make room for your expansion of yourself. No two energies can occupy the same space. As you move out of old energy fields, you make more room to expand into the new and now of you. As you continue to let go of old, worn-out belief systems, it is most important to let go of any material substances that may have a past connection to the beliefs.

Eventually, you will expand into freedom. You will become the beautiful butterfly of many colors that brings beauty to others and the world. Freedom of the Soul for yourself, others, and your great Mother Earth will be what is most important to you. The way you want to experience this freedom will be totally different for you. You will not be seeing the world and its evolution through the Shadow or duality lens. Your experience will be one of total love and acceptance. You will truly love thy neighbor as yourself because you will know and feel that you are your neighbor.

There is only love, and as your vibration is love, that will be your experience of all existence. This is the new paradigm you are moving into. As co-creators, you think your desires in thought, and they will manifest very quickly because there is no separation between you and what you desire. You are energy, and all is you.

You are in one of the best places of consciousness that has

ever taken place on your planet. As the old structures break down, you, the light ones, will find yourselves connecting to greater aspects of yourselves spiritually. You will once again come together in community. You will find much bartering and sharing happening. You will use your connection to Spirit to once again manifest your dreams.

Many, many Souls who never would have looked for themselves will start to pray. Their beginning spiritual journey will be out of fear, yet the outcome will be one of love, love of self and others. The old structures must break loose to be able to build a new future for yourself and future generations.

Soul groups will find each other again and bring their gifts together. Remember, you each have a piece of the puzzle. As you come back and put your pieces together, you will create a complete puzzle. You will awaken into the wholeness within yourself individually and collectively.

# MOVING OUT OF THE I ME
# AND INTO THE
# I AM

*"Where the intention goes, the energy flows."*

Your Souls are hungry. They are crying to be fed. They do not want more materialism; they want freedom. Free me. Love me. Free me. I want to go home again. You need not leave the planet to come home. Your agreement is to come home within yourself on the Earth plane to co-create Heaven on Earth.

As old structures are breaking down, this is happening: You are awakening. You are thinking for yourselves. What is important to me? How do I feel about this? What do I want for myself, my world and future generations?

I want you to think about what I am saying to you. In the past, when a Soul of you had financial security, you felt safe. Your life was working, and you could feed your children and educate them. You could go on vacations and have fun.

In the realm of thinking and experiencing, your world was quite small. Many of you did not know or understand that across your world, children were going hungry. Souls/Cells/People did not have homes or schooling, and their basic needs were not even being met.

As your secure structures are being torn down, you are expanding yourself beyond old beliefs and perceptions. You are starting to think and ask why. How could this happen? You are truly waking up and taking your power back. You are unthreading from the old perceptions of security.

You are now moving out of the I ME and into the I AM. Your expansion of self is now beyond you and your security and into the larger picture of life, of others and your world.

As your old security continues to break apart, you will find yourself awakening into more conscious aspects of yourself. Light bulbs will constantly go on. You will find that you have a voice. Your perceptions will continually change. As your perceptions change, your choices in life become more conscious. As your choices become more conscious, the energy of this higher thought intention spreads through the world and connects with other Souls of the same intention and frequency.

This connection energetically moves you into a higher consciousness collectively. This collective thought intention is so powerful and strong it lifts the whole consciousness into a higher frequency. Remember, your intention creates your reality and world. As you vibrate together in a higher intent, you are energetically forming a new agreement for the better of other Souls/Cells and your world.

Where the attention goes the energy flows. As you are all creation, when you set a higher intention, you realign with Me, My highest consciousness, and together We will heal your world. We will co-create Heaven on Earth. Your thinking will be one with Me. You will constantly evolve, awakening into a greater consciousness of the I AM.

You are not alone; you have never been. You cannot heal and change your world without Me, and I cannot do this without you. You are going through a death of old belief systems and separation and moving into the birth of Ascension and enlightenment.

Thought is powerful! Align your thoughts with My I AM

of All That Is, which is you in your highest form. Become one with Me so that We can quickly move the consciousness of your world and all of the Souls of your world into Ascension and enlightenment. My greatest desire for you is to live in Heaven on your Earth plane, and for all of you to remember how much I love you. I created you as Me, and I love all aspects of you, for you are Me.

When I look at all of Creation, I marvel at the magnificence of All That Is. How could I not love what I have created? All of this Creation is I. I love My Creation of I. You are My Creation, and I love you as much as I love Myself, for you are Me.

When you put in your call to the I AM of Me, I know that you are ready to remember who you are. When this happens, you will find yourself starting to vibrate in serendipity.

All in life mirrors you, and you always bring people, places, things, events, and circumstances into your life to assist you to heal, grow, and remember your magnificence. Just when you feel your life is starting to go well, you may bring someone into your life who will mirror your old emotional patterns. When this happens, you will feel shattered. Old feelings that you have denied will surface and will throw you back into the core of the pattern.

When you are in the core of the pattern, you become the pattern again. You see and experience life once again through this emotional fear bondage.

You must bring all of your bodies into balance with harmonizing frequencies and vibrations. You will not be able to move forward in your Souls' highest agreement until you balance your bodies out.

Your unloved emotional body will control and affect your

mental, physical, cellular, and etheric bodies. Your unhealed emotional body runs through all of your systems. It will thread through your body and eventually take over. If you are a mental, or left-brained, person, you may not even know that it is happening because you are not in touch with your feelings.

If not healed, your unhealed emotional body gets your attention through sickness and dis-ease.

This dis-ease starts changing your perspective. As I said, this change of perspective starts changing your life, or awakening you into life's meaning. The dis-ease becomes your wake-up call to find yourself. If you allow it, the dis-ease begins your journey home inside yourself, or if you waited too long, home into Spirit.

I ask that you honor your emotions. Love them, give them a voice, and set them free so that all of your bodies can harmonize in peace, love, joy, abundance, and hope. Whatever the question, love is the answer.

# ASCENSION: HEALING YOUR WORLD BY CHANGING YOUR THOUGHTS

*"Change your thoughts, and you change your world."*

I wish to speak to you of Ascension. Ascension is moving all of your bodies into a higher frequency of Me, the I AM of All That Is. When the Soul of you is in the Ascension of the I AM, you are actually activating memories within your cellular structure, which allow the light-sound of you to move you into another time frame. To ascend means to move beyond linear time.

When one ascends, you move through all karmic lifetimes and agreements back into the highest consciousness of your I AM. This is a time of great change in your life and in the lives of all around you. As you continue to awaken out of linear time, you start awakening all of the Souls in other bodies who you interact with on the Earth plane.

Because you are each other, when the coding in your DNA is activated and you move to a higher frequency, you open the doorway for all Souls to follow. An actual portal beyond time opens, and you start moving through the veils of illusion within yourself. As you continue to shed the veils, you start moving through the dimensions that the veil is connected to.

As this happens, an expansion of your I ME self starts connecting with your I AM multi-dimensionally. This happens individually and collectively. Your collective consciousness unthreads from the karmic collective and starts reconnecting energetically with aspects of yourself that are already awakened and enlightened.

You must be enlightened before you totally ascend. This does not mean that you cannot move through the veils of illusion into higher frequencies of yourself, through the Ascension process.

To change the old, karmic patterns, you must change your thoughts, which changes their frequencies. You do this by setting the intention for the outcome to be different. You then do something different by which the pattern will be confused.

Take a different route; create a new route for your light to travel through. Do not be angry with or fight against your Ego. If you do, you continue to feed it, stimulate it, and empower it.

You want to disempower it! You do this by loving yourself enough to want your life to become easier and happier.

Do this by taking a different road. If you are used to walking down a certain path, take a different one.

If you always do what you always did, you always get what you always got. You have to do it differently for the outcome to be different. As I explained, patterns become their own entity and are very predictable. To change the pattern, it is important to confuse it.

If you always drive your car down the same road at the same time to the same destination, you will always go to the same place. Take a different road, a different route. Go on a different journey. Allow this journey to be one of self-empowerment.

What is not love is fear, and the Ego Shadow has a great fear of death, individually and collectively.

Remember; do not respond to the Ego. Thank it for sharing, and put it to bed.

*Instead of re-acting in anger, go into the center of your golden heart. When someone upsets you, breathe and take yourself and the emotion into the center of your golden heart. If you have fear, imagine placing the fear into the center of your golden heart. You will feel it break up and dissipate.*

*Thank your Ego for sharing. Tell it you have learned much from it. Wrap it into a blanket of the golden Christ energy, and bring it into the core, or center, of your golden heart, which is in alignment with the Central Sun's energy. This will send golden Christ energy into the Ego. Remember, the Ego has no power on its own. It feeds off your old fear patterns.*

*Take a few deep breaths, and breathe into the center of your golden heart. Through continual practice, your subconscious will know to surrender into the center of your golden heart. Through this practice, you will re-trace and re-thread yourself through time into the collective I Am. You will feel great peace and love within yourself, and your perspective of life will change because you will no longer be sending out mixed duality messages.*

Do not be afraid of bringing energies into your heart that you perceive as negative. You are bringing aspects of yourself into the core of your own Christ love. As you do this, the fear-based pattern, or incident, starts breaking up, dissipating, and transmuting to love. You will feel your own love expand and become stronger.

This will feel like a stone being thrown into the water. You will feel ripples of love, of light, move through your bodies and systems. You will feel yourself quieter and floating into peace. **Change your thoughts, and you change your world!!!**

If you allow yourself to constantly bring the Golden Sun into your heart and allow it to be your hearts' constant vibration, you will feel yourself going deeper into your own self-love and into the center of your Souls' I AM. You will experience yourself more and more in love with self.

From this self-love, your reflection of others will be love. Love, joy, and happiness will be your constant companions, for there is no separation between you and your environment. It is up to you as to which frequency you choose to vibrate in: love or fear.

You can also choose to bring the Golden Sun into the back of your heart, as well as the front. You will feel both sides connect into the center core of your heart. This will feel like an energy that expands you beyond time. It is a very quick way to bring your vibration to a higher level. You will experience this golden light expand through all of your bodies until your etheric body is so filled with the golden light that you feel like a safe child within yourself.

This will quicken you into the light of Ascension, which will activate codings in your DNA of a higher consciousness of your Being.

# CO-CREATING A NEW LIFETIME

*"You are coming into a new lifetime on the Earth*
*without physically leaving the body."*

It is most important that you bring all aspects of yourself into the now. It is almost impossible to do this if you have not allowed yourself to surrender into your emotions.

You must be willing to let go and die. It is important to surrender into your greatest fears. As you allow yourself to do this, you are going through a karmic death.

I am not saying to you that this is easy. As you surrender into your greatest fears, you start losing who you think you are, who you think you are supposed to be, and other Souls' programs of who you are and who they think you are. You start shedding your old identity.

When your old identity breaks up or you break through your old illusional perceptions of yourself, you start discovering the truth of who you are, which is My greatest love of all, for you are Me. You cannot miss it because it is.

In the center of your core is the magnificent light of Creation, which is who you are. This light is the total balance and love of the highest aspects of Me, which are you. In this balance, you and your higher self will start merging together in your higher understanding into Knowingness.

You are coming into a new lifetime on the Earth without physically leaving the body.

I see many spontaneous enlightenments happening to you great Souls of Me on your planet Earth. As you are ascending and moving into higher aspects of yourself, your cells are activating memories in you that have already been enlightened. Because like attracts like, when this happens, you turn on that vibration within yourself, and when the two lights connect, you wake up and remember who you are.

In this new lifetime, you need a new family unit. This new family unit is Me and your Mother Sophia. Your biological parents will always be your Earth parents in this lifetime, but your intention is to complete karmically with Them. From a place of love, you will release the contracts of what needed to be learned with Them, and will move into alignment with the higher aspects of the collective I Am consciousness.

From this higher consciousness, it is important to write a new contract. This contract is the intention of your life now on the planet.

Through the spoken word, release old karmic contracts and emotions.

Say out loud:

*I now set the intention to be totally done with all past lifetimes. I release the karmic collective consciousness of all lifetimes, all programs, contracts, belief systems, patterns, emotions of anger, rage, resentment, fear, mistrust of God, of Spirit, of love.*

*I release all karmic contracts connected to these emotions that are in my heart, thymus, throat, third eye, crown, spine, root, sexual organs, my second chakra and solar plexus, past, present, future in any way, shape or form.*

*I release the karmic collective consciousness and
all contracts of separation and control by churches,
religions, governments, karma, belief systems, cultures,
prejudice, and projections of fear by the Shadow.*

*I release all programs of fear projections, all implants,
microchips and all reversed programming that are in
my heart, throat, third eye, crown, root, sexual organs,
second chakra and solar plexus and in my mental,
emotional, physical cellular and etheric bodies, past,
present and future. I Am love. I Am light, only love,
only light. I Am. I Am. I Am.*

*Remember the importance of forgiveness and
release. I forgive and release Mother, Father God,
and Creation. I forgive and release my parents
and ancestors from all lifetimes and agreements. I
forgive and release the imbalance of my male and
female, of my heart and Ego, of my light and Shadow.
I forgive and release the crucifixion of Christ, of
the Christ consciousness. I forgive and release the
violation and rape of the feminine, of the fear, control
and denial and competition with the feminine and
between the feminine. I forgive and release everyone
and everything. I forgive and release everyone and
everything. I forgive myself. I forgive and release*

*myself. I forgive myself and I ask that all forgive me. I*
*trust and believe that the consciousness has changed*
*and I am now safe to be the innocence of my child, to be*
*the highest love and light of my I AM*
*and to live my highest spiritual purpose now.*
*I AM. I AM. I AM. I AM.*

Even if you don't think or believe that you have anyone or anything to forgive, saying these words of forgiveness will vibrate through all dimensions of you and release any old fragmented thought forms, or patterns, that may still be influencing you in any negative way.

Any time you release, you must reaffirm the highest of who you are. All is energy, and the space emptied must be filled back up with positive energy. As you go through this verbal release, you will feel the energy releasing from your bodies. You will feel lighter and freer, making room for more love and light to fill your bodies.

Look at all patterns in your life. Go through a verbal release of them through all chakras and bodies. (Remember the power of the spoken word.) Any pattern that you come into this lifetime to break through has a frame of reference elsewhere. As you move the energy through the now out of your systems, the thought, or intention, connects to the memories stored in your cells and system from the old reference point and releases it also.

After you go through this energetic release, move yourself back into the center of your heart, the Golden Christ energy. From your heart, send this love frequency through your bodies, and your subconscious will unlock your unconscious and will immediately start downloading the love energy into your cells and tissues.

If you continue to allow yourself to use the word to release, your subconscious will recognize and remember the process and will know it is time to fill you back up with light. Your subconscious will work with you in the light and will download your super-consciousness of My I AM into you.

In this new lifetime, it is important to set up a balance support of Me that is you. This is the total balance of the male and female.

As I was explaining, after any release you must fill yourself back up with the highest consciousness of love. Ask for your spiritual mother, Sophia, to fill your Being with Her feminine love and light. Ask Her to fill your bodies up with the feminine mother's love and light. As you do this, you will create a new system of support beyond any karmic agreements. Then wait and allow Her to respond. You will feel a peace and sense of safety fill your whole Being with light. Open the communication with Her. Ask Her what she wants to say to you. The message will come through your mind. At first, you may think it is you talking to yourself. The more you do this, the more you will feel Her energy. Then, when you ask for a message, you will feel Her energy blend into you through the message.

If you are not sure it is Her and you have the knowledge of muscle testing your body, do the testing because your body will not lie to you. If you do not receive the message at first because you cannot feel Her energy, continue to ask and Her love and light connected to your intention will open the lines of communication.

When you can start feeling the energy, you may receive the message through feelings, through the Knowingness of the energy. As you feel Her, you may just know what the message is without Her verbally speaking to you.

After you bring the feminine mother to you, ask for Me, your father, to be with you. Ask and you shall receive. Ask for your inner father, the I Am of All That Is, and you will feel My essence fill your whole Being. You will feel a sense of strength, confidence and safety. Then ask if I have a message for you. Open the lines of communication with Me, for I am you and I love you. Bring Me, your real father, to you as the guardian parent of love and light. I am the patriarchal energy that your Cells and Souls know as true safety and love.

I want to assist you to remember and feel the Creation of yourself in love. As you move into this new lifetime, I want to be your new foundation. I Am your divine Father and Mother. Connect with Me, and you will feel a love and safety that you have never experienced before. Allow Me to be your guiding light and constant confidante.

I, the balance of the highest Creation of the male and female, will now guide you and keep you safe to assist in co-creating Heaven on Earth. We are one; We have never been separate. You just forgot. Allow your whole Being of the I AM self to re-thread with Me.

I love you. I am you. You are Me. And so it is.

# BUILDING A NEW FOUNDATION
# IN THIS NEW LIFETIME

*"You all have a little girl and a little boy inside of you*
*waiting to be given permission to awaken, to feel safe*
*enough to open up and remember their own love."*

Begin each day with the love of your parents, the balanced male and female, Mother and Father of Me. Start your day with the connection of your higher self. Begin your day tuned in beyond duality. Allow yourself to be constantly guided and directed by becoming one with your higher self and the highest Mother and Father's love. Ask for your higher self's connection. Then bring your inner Mother and Father of Me, the I AM, to you. You will feel safe, secure, and divinely supported as you move through your day. Your new foundation will be set.

Next bring your inner children to you. You all have a little girl and little boy inside of you waiting to be given permission to awaken, to feel safe enough to open up and remember their own love. Only you, the adult, can give this to them. The feminine is your inner girl, your spirituality, your love-light feeling of Me. The male, your inner boy, is your mind, your will, and the aspect of self that goes forward and is also the love and light of Me. Many times, your inner children, your little girl and boy, do not have a conscious memory of one another. You need both the male and female to go forward. They are your innocence and when they feel safe, they will re-awaken to the understanding and knowing love, of all that is.

It is important, that as you make the connection to each one of them individually and they start feeling safe inside of you, that you introduce them to each another. Many times they do not remember that the other one exists. They are each other, the balance of one another, the heart and the mind. As you bring them back together within yourself, they will feel loved and safe together. You, the adult, will then start feeling loved and safe because you experience all of your life through the emotions of your inner children. If they are hurt, you, the adult, will feel their hurt emotions. If they feel safe, you, the adult, will feel safe.

It is most important that once you have made the contact with them, that you stay connected.

*Talk to them. Let them know how much you love them. Tell them that they are safe now, that they are one with their real parents, Mother-Father God-Creator. Bring Sophia's and My love through your heart and into theirs. Run the infinity energy through their hearts. Bring Our energy through your hands and into them. Hold them in Our love. Give them everything you needed but may not have received as a child from your biological parents. As they start healing and growing up emotionally, they will start feeling happy, more joyous, and safe. Safety is a big issue for your inner children. As they start feeling better, you, the adult will, because your emotions are theirs; you are them.*

*Make a conscious connection to them every morning so they know that you will always be there for them. You will not abandon them. Re-assure them that you love them and they are now safe with you. They will know and feel that no one will ever hurt them again.*

I hear some of you say, "but that is such a great responsibility, how can I keep them safe when I don't trust or feel safe myself?" You do this by moving out of the "I ME" and into the "I AM," by becoming one with your higher self, with your inner Mother Sophia and with Me, your Father. You then have a strong spiritual foundation to assist you to move beyond your Earthly story and into the larger picture of your purpose. Because your children are still very connected to Spirit, from this place they will feel loved and safe. The veils of illusion will lift from them, and they will once again feel their innocence and safety with Us. When you connect to them daily and give them permission, they will reconnect with Me and your Mother. As they feel this inner safety net of Love, this Love will ripple back into you, the adult.

# GIVING BIRTH TO YOUR INNER CRYSTAL CHILDREN

*"Your inner children are your road map to freedom. Your inner children carry the road map (karmic contract) of all that is needed to be understood, healed, released, and forgiven."*

Every thing, event, and situation that has happened to you in this lifetime that you are now coming out of has a past life or another frame of reference to it. You agreed to go through the lesson again to release the karmic emotions connected to it.

Inside your karmic children are your Crystal Children who are waiting to be acknowledged, recognized, and embraced. Your Inner Crystal Children are now ready to be birthed by you with Sophia and I as your family unit of love, light and safety.

These inner children of you are the seeds of your future generation, and they are the future of your world. They are holding the frequency for you, the adult, to awaken and bring forth the Crystal Children within you. The time is now for the collective Crystal consciousness to be rethreaded. You are these Crystal Children. You went before, moved through, and opened the karmic gateways for the Crystal Beings of light who are coming through now. Their agreement with you is to hold the light for the rebirth of your Crystal consciousness within you to emerge. You have been the guiding light for them, and as you have come full circle into a new lifetime within yourself, they are now the guiding light for you to become one with them to carry the consciousness through portals of light into your New World.

Their vibration alone will heal your world if they are supported in their mission. They come from the future and are here to tune the vibration of you and your world to a higher octave of sound and light.

They will mirror back to all their own magnificence and light. They are the highest teachers that have come to your planet. Their frequency is so high that they could not have been born on the planet before the time of now. The consciousness of the planet was not high enough to hold the light for them. They would have been blown out energetically.

As I said, within each of you, your Crystal Children are now waiting to be born. The importance of me speaking to you of your inner children is that they are the collective Second Coming of the Christ energy.

After you have built your foundation with Sophia and I, as the love and safety of your inner parents, ask for your Crystal Children to come to you. Remember, inside your karmic child is your Crystal Child waiting to be born.

*Take your Crystal Children through the same process as you did with your karmic children. Imagine a divine little girl in your heart. Communicate to her. Let her know how much you love her, how much she is wanted, and how valuable and important she is to you. Give her everything that you feel you did not get with your biological parents.*

*Feel the love of your Inner Parents of Me, of My heart's love, move out through your heart and into the heart and body of your new Crystal Child. Talk to her, love her and re-assure her that she is now safe to awaken and emerge.*

*As she feels totally loved, safe and secure, you, the adult, will because you experience all life through the emotions of your inner children. When they feel loved, safe, and secure, you, the adult, will because you are them. Your inner crystal children will activate and turn the light on within you of your highest spiritual knowing.*

*Now, do the same process with your crystal inner boy. Ask for a divine Being of light to hand your little boy to you. Hold him against your heart with your little girl. Love him and reassure him that he is safe to awaken and emerge into light.*

*Bring the love and light through your heart and hands into the little boy, sending a light frequency into him that runs through his heart and links him to the little girl's heart. Again, imagine the infinity energy running through both of their hearts. Now bring your karmic children together with your Crystal Children. The light of your Crystal Children will start penetrating your karmic children. Eventually they will blend together in higher consciousness as one Child of Light. As I said, inside of each karmic child is the Crystal Child waiting to be born. As you bring them together daily, the programming of the karmic child dissolves into light. As this happens, the veils release and the karmic child awakens into the enlightened Crystal Child.*

*Give them all an identity. They all carry different sound vibrations of your personality. When you first connect to your Inner Children, ask them what they want to be called; it may be different than your given name. If they don't tell you their names, give them the names with which you feel comfortable. Remember, all names have a color-sound frequency vibration. As you bring them together in balance, love and harmony, you the adult will feel this throughout your bodies. You are then building a new lifetime for yourself of total balance of the male's and female's love and light on all levels.*

*Start communicating with your inner Crystal Children daily. They will give you much information that the adult aspects of yourself have forgotten.*

Your Crystal Children are total consciousness and will guide you with their enlightened wisdom. If you feel stuck in your life, ask them to tell you what is happening. Because they are still at one with God, the Source, they can tell you what the problem is that is keeping you stuck. They are in the higher understanding, or picture, of all stories. Your crystal children will assist you, the adult, to vibrate throughout your cells in the higher vibration of your Souls' Sound and Song.

You will truly feel at home within yourself and will vibrate in the Crystal frequency, mirroring to others the light of their own songs and sounds. **And so it is.**

# CO-CREATING A NEW WORLD

*"Now is the time to co-create with Me the love and joy of life, which is your birthright."*

In the beginning, there was the word, and the word was love. My word is still the way home through the heart.

When the consciousness on your planet was re-awakening, a structure needed to be formed. The structure was the word of I, the Father.

You have had many incarnations on the Earth plane, where you came to an end of what your Soul could comprehend, or understand, at the time.

There was no failure and never has been. You played out end times of the opposition between the heart and Ego. When that was done, in whatever form it took, the civilization came to an end, and you moved back home with Me to understand the whole play. All of your incarnations have been plays so that you and the collective could act out and release any illusions, or misunderstandings, of Me that you were still vibrating in.

When the play came to an end and you moved back into Spirit with Me, you were able to look at the lifetime that you were coming out of as if you were watching a movie. It was then that you could experience yourself clearly. Because you received many impressions from your Earth parents, surroundings, and environments, you were then able to see clearly how these influences orchestrated your life's decisions.

From the play becoming very clear, you chose to reincarnate to the Earth again and re-write your new script, to complete the lessons that your Soul needed to learn or did not complete.

When you were able to see all of the movies that you made from your agreed upon lifetimes, which kept you in fear-based realities, you became more conscious in re-writing the new script for your next lifetime.

As I speak to you now, it is to give you My word anew. My greatest desire is to bring you back home to Me through My love for you.

My heart, arms, mind, and the higher consciousness of Me is open to you to remember who you are so that you can return to Me, within yourself, within your heart, within self-love.

Every role that could possibly be played out, you have already played. You need not struggle to remember who you are. There is no need to play the villain or victim to understand duality. You are every experience. You have great wisdom and knowledge within yourself.

Now is the time of great awakening. I am calling all of you home to Me. Your job of duality is done. You have served this great awakening well. Collectively, all that needs to be known is known. This Knowingness now has to be brought forth into the light, into your own light.

As I am gathering all of My children to come home to Me and into the heart of My beloved Sophia, We are shining a light so brightly that your path home, through the heart, through love, will be much easier.

Much of the disturbance on your planet now is because of the light frequencies of My I AM are penetrating all of your fear illusions. This light is shattering the Shadow within you and the collective.

You are in a death and re-birth cycle at the same time.

I say to you, set your intention. You have a beautiful,

brilliant mind. Use this mind in alignment with My mind and heart. We will co-create a civilization so brilliantly light that the light will dissipate all confusing illusion.

Now is the time to co-create with Me, the love and joy of life that is your birthright. You were born of Me and are still Me. My greatest desire is to mirror My love and light back to you so strongly that all on your planet will have spontaneous enlightenment. I want all of you to remember your own magnificence.

You are the mind and heart of Me, and I love you.

Your planet can quickly evolve out of separation from My highest if you set the intention for this to happen. Thought is energy, and when all set their intention, through the feeling of your heart's love, to have a better world, I, your Father and Mother, will align My heart and intent with yours. We will co-create Heaven on Earth in all life forms.

I am now sending light frequencies to your planet. You and the Mother Earth are in your birth canal of Ascension, of Enlightenment.

The light is coming down in about two-month intervals, or 60-day cycles, opening portals of consciousness within you and throughout all Creations. In days to come, these cycles will become much shorter. You are moving into monthly and weekly cycles and eventually daily. Any light cycle activates codings, or portals, of light in your DNA that bring you into a higher consciousness of awakening, perceiving, and understanding within yourself.

Every time this birth contraction happens, you are moving through the womb of Creation and into a higher light of the I AM of All That Is.

When the light hits, you will feel many old feelings and emotions surface so that you can go through them and pull the roots up. Your feelings and emotions are from every incarnation, individually and collectively.

Through this great awakening, you might feel uncomfortable within yourselves. You will sometimes feel nauseous and have vertigo, and your bodies will feel out of balance. You will be losing your identity of who you thought you were, or what you thought you were supposed to be.

Goals that you had set for yourself may no longer seem real or important. You will have great confusion and feel like you are losing your memory. Your taste for food will change. You will not know what you want to eat. Nothing will taste good. As your vibration is being turned up, you must put higher vibrational foods and energies into your systems. Your bodies need food as energy or fuel. You must bring into your bodies the food that vibrates with now.

All of your bodies are losing their old memories and need to know that all is well. Talk to your bodies as you would a child. Let them know that you love them and honor them. Thank them for being a beautiful home for you in this lifetime.

Acknowledge your beautiful bodies. They need to be loved and honored just as you, the adult, does. As you acknowledge your beautiful bodies, they will feel very peaceful, loved and grateful that they now have the opportunity to be free.

Your bodies carry all of the memories of your mind and need much love and support. Love them to health and into their optimum potential.

You may have days when you have great energy and then the next day none. You will feel like you are on a roller coaster ride.

Go with the ride. Go with the flow. Your bodies are detoxifying and re-adjusting to the new vibration, if you need to rest or sleep, set time aside to do this. Be in the moment of now. Act from now.

Who you were in the past is gone. Live in the now. Do not judge yourself for what you are feeling or going through. Love yourself. Accept yourself. Honor yourself, and be kind and gentle with yourself. Honor yourself for your willingness to come to planet Earth and for being a part of this great awakening now. See your cup as full instead of empty.

No one has failed. You are on the Earth again with all of your fellow travelers to become totally awakened.

You agreed to come to the Earth with other great Souls with a wiped slate, clean of all memories of enlightenment, or Ascension.

You went into the depth of the Shadow collectively. You agreed to begin totally unconscious and very quickly moved through the karmic wheels collectively to re-awaken all consciousness into light of enlightenment, or Ascension.

Jeshua was the Being of My light who agreed to reincarnate to your planet and open the door for the Christ that is you, to awaken. You are Me and the Christed ones. You are the Second Coming of Christ. The golden light on your planet is very bright. You are in the Golden Age, the Second Coming, and within your DNA systems are codes that are now being activated.

These codes are of My highest Creation of you. Every time one of My light frequencies hits your planet, the light activates the coding in your DNA individually and collectively of the Second Coming of the I AM of All That Is, and lifts you into a higher frequency of the Golden Ray of consciousness.

The Golden Ray is Ascension, enlightenment, and peace on Earth. This is love, happiness, joy, freedom, and abundance on all levels. The Second Coming is all Souls/Cells of My light and love coming together home on the Earth plane, co-creating Heaven on Earth. This is living in the true Garden of Eden, in My Golden Temple, in the Heart of all knowing, of Oneness, of Grace.

# SELF-REALIZATION – THROUGH INTENTION

*"Your intentions will continue to change and expand as your perceptions become higher consciousness of Me."*

Now is the time to set your intention. Thought is energy. You, the light rays, lead the way for many others to find their way through the darkness and home to Me. Think as you, the collective rays of light, come together in Oneness, the light will be so bright that it will open the passageway for many Souls/ Cells of you to move through the portals and back into their I AM selves.

Come together in Soul Groups and set your intentions collectively. Bring your hearts, love, light, and songs back together. Create beautiful harmony to soothe and heal your whole world.

Thought is energy! Co-create a new paradigm. Hold this frequency for all to connect with and vibrate in. This new consciousness will penetrate the hearts and Cells of the other Cells/Souls of you.

They will feel hope. This hope will give them energy to move through the doorway, or birth canal, into the Golden Age of innocence.

As you come together in groups, set your intentions collectively. After your Soul Group's intention is set, put this collective intention into Our Golden Hearts and expand them through all consciousness. Other Cells will feel it and will vibrate higher collectively.

This thought energy intention is your inner core vibration of love and light. As your intention is to expand it through the Golden Heart, Central Sun's energy, it will weave itself into the cellular structures of Cells/Souls of the same color-light-sound frequency.

As you collectively move into a higher vibration of light and sound, the sound will break loose old, frozen emotional patterns, or grid systems. When these old patterns start breaking loose, it is most important to hold the intention to create a new grid system, or paradigm, collectively.

When an old emotional pattern breaks, a new frequency must be downloaded in its place. Hold the frequency until the collective subconscious accepts the love and light frequency as its new truth.

Be firm in your intention. This is creating a safety net for all to realize that they are safe in love and light. The collective subconscious needs to remember that its true nature is this highest love and light of Me, the I AM of All That Is.

Your intentions will continue to change and expand as your perceptions become higher consciousness of Me. Do not be confused by this. As your consciousness becomes higher, so do your perceptions, which create your intentions.

I love you, for you are Me. I honor you for your agreements to go to the Earth and to bring yourselves into Self-Realization, Enlightenment and Ascension, collectively. Now is the time you have been waiting for since the beginning of the great illusion of separation. You have never been separate. You have been taking a nap. Now you are waking up together as Me, the I AM, through all Creations. You are remembering who you are. You are magnificent Beings of My light, love and Creation. We are not separate; We have always been and will always be.

As you continue your journey home inside of your heart and Soul of Me, you will feel yourself in the sunrise of all consciousness understanding. The unconscious will become conscious for you. You will vibrate in total Knowingness, which is the Oneness of Me beyond the duality fear illusion.

I have waited for you and assisted you each step of the way, as you have assisted Me.

Open your hearts to My golden love, that is you. Continue to surrender into love, for love is All That Is. Allow this love to permeate your whole Being. It is the power that will lift mountains and dissipate all old fear-based frequencies.

You are great masters of My I AM. Many of My great teachers and Masters have walked on your planet and prepared the foundation to open the door for your brother Jeshua. Now you are the Masters who are preparing and holding open the doorways of the Golden Light for others.

As many walked before you, you are now walking before others of you. You are the wayshowers of the Golden Age of Ascension.

Walk humbly, My children. Know who you are. Walk with great love, peace, and grace in your heart. Know that all is you, and the more you love yourself, the more you can love and accept others of you. Know that I am you and am always walking with you, and I am continuing to shower My great light upon you to show you your way home.

If you are in loneliness, go into your Golden Heart Temple. Go inside yourself, and you will know Me, for I am you. Once inside your Golden Temple, ask and you will receive. My gift to you now is for you to consciously know Me, as you, in your love and magnificence.

Manifest yourself as the co-creator of Me. Do this by going into your Golden Heart Temple and expand yourself through all Creations of Me, that are you. This light will assist you to feel a higher vibration of My love for you. You will feel great peace and comfort. You will feel like a child wrapped in a golden blanket. Open your hearts and minds and talk to Me. Open the energy lines of communication with Me. I love you. You are My child, My children, My great, great, grand-children of love.

My greatest desire is for you to know My love for you. I want you to feel safe with Me so that you can intend yourself into co-creation of the highest good, for yourself and all mankind.

If you ask, you will receive. You may not feel My answer at first, but the more you communicate with Me, the more you will feel My frequency. As you do this, you will move into direct communication with Me. I will speak to you. I will shower My love on you. I will show you your way home. I am your guiding light. I AM. I AM. I AM.

# I AM

*"I am every thread and vibration of existence. I am the
vibration of every cell in your body. I am all Creation.
How you decide to use Me is up to you."*

I AM. I AM. I AM. I am the trees, the birds, the springtime
of your life and consciousness.

I am death and rebirth. I am the wintertime of your life. I
come at unexpected times, and I take the jewels from your
life to assist you into a higher understanding or unveiling of
yourself. I AM All That Is; all that is constant, death and rebirth, winding down and rebuilding, awakening.

Your whole lifetime now and all lifetimes have been a
continuous cycle of death and rebirth. Death is a closure to
one experience, and rebirth is the next step past the closure.

There is truly no death, only constant rebirth. As you come
to an end of a chosen experience, you either learn the lesson or
not, but you always come to a closure of the chosen agreement.

Sometimes, the closure means you must leave the body to
go on the next adventure of your Soul's journey. Some Souls
cycle very quickly. Others take more time to grow, understand,
and complete before moving to the next required experience.
All experiences that all Souls have agreed to go through are
to understand, release, and to free themselves from karmic
emotions, to move back into the core of My Beingness, of the
I AM of All That Is!

I AM All That Is, and all that is not. I am every breath
you take and every breath you do not take. I am every thread

and vibration of existence. I am the vibration of every cell in your body. I am all Creation. How you decide to use Me is up to you. You can use Me in all of My light power and existence, or you can use Me to feed and empower your pain, your Shadow.

I am your laughter and joy. I am your fear, sorrows, and regrets. I AM All That Is. Nothing exists without Me. I am the core of your existence. I am your Mother-Father God-Creation. I am the frequency, the mind and the heart of God awakened into you. I am the bloom of all knowing, as I am the total bloom of you.

I am the sun and the moon. I am all elements. I am the Earth and the stars. I am all cultures and all religions. I am new beginnings and old endings. I am the wind. I am the ocean. I am the water, and I am the air that you breathe. Without Me, you cannot exist. I am all Creation.

You see and experience All That Is through your perceptions of Me. Your perceptions of Me come from your direct experience of all collective emotions. You could not hold on to your old perceptions if you did not have others to align, agree, or mirror back to you your perceptions.

You are in a holographic consciousness. As I exist throughout all consciousness, you exist through all consciousness. You could not see yourself, or know yourself, without Me, for you are Me. I am the life force in all existence. You could not know yourself if you did not have the Shadow aspect of My I AM, to mirror back to you, your reflection of light.

You could not know your Shadow without your light. You could not know your light without your Shadow. All of I AM needs polarization to balance all consciousness of Me. I AM.

The I AM frequency of your planet is now in the highest light-sound vibration that has ever been. This frequency is turned up beyond the original template of the Shadow-sound frequency.

This is what is happening on your planet now. The old template that held the groove of your existence on your planet is worn out. Your I AM consciousness has been stuck in the old sound-music template. You and I, the collective I AM, have turned the vibration up high enough to move the needle of the I AM beyond the template frequencies.

This agreed-upon happening is moving you beyond any time zone where you have believed or experienced yourself vibrating in separateness. My I AM frequency is moving you, all light and Shadow aspects of yourself, beyond time.

You are now coexisting and vibrating in all dimensions simultaneously. You are now vibrating with yourself in parallel realities, universes, and lifetimes. All I AM is coming together, and your light-sound I AM frequencies are breaking loose all old beliefs, fears, and perceptions.

If you could see My I AM in all consciousness, both light and Shadow and all beautiful color-sound frequencies in between, you would be able to experience yourself in all of your glory, for all is you. I AM the glue that holds you together. I AM the emptiness in your heart waiting to once again be filled up with love.

When you see all as Me, you see all of who you are. You are powerful Beingness of My I AM. I ask you once again to vibrate in your highest I AM Knowingness. In this I AM comes total magnificence. You know all in total love and acceptance, for all is you.

I know you, for I AM you. I love you, for I AM you. I see you, for I AM you. I AM. I AM. I AM. I AM the I AM of All That Is!

# ABOUT THE AUTHOR

**Michelle Phillips** is an internationally renowned intuitive, healer, speaker, teacher and workshop facilitator. She has appeared on various radio and TV shows worldwide. For over 5 years she was the host of the very popular live call-in spiritual television show, "Soul's Awakening." She was the co-host of the radio show "Soul's Purpose Salon" and while living in Northern California, she started the monthly "Spiritual Connection Breakfast."

Michelle was born conscious of her gifts and always had a direct connection to the Source. She began her conscious spiritual work in the early 70's after healing her son from a severe kidney ailment. Since that Spiritual Awakening, she has dedicated her life to her spiritual purpose and mission, assisting others in their Soul's Awakening, self-love and purpose; co-creating Heaven on Earth in all life forms.

She refers to Christ as "Her Main Man." He has been with her, assisting and teaching her from a young age and has taught Michelle her spiritual work through her own healing experiences.

Michelle has been referred to as an Inter-Galactic Shaman because of her knowledge and ability to travel through many dimensions: Light-Dark, Shadow, Above and Below. She is known as the Healer's Healer. Many people come to Michelle as a last resort, when everything else has failed, and from her work they experience life-changing transformations.

**Her work includes:**

- Workshops
- Soul-Readings ~ Past Life Regression ~ Soul Retrieval ~ Higher Self-Integration
- Inner Child Therapy ~ Childhood Trauma
- Relationship Issues ~ Twin-Flame Healing of Imbalance
- Emotional Healings ~ Addiction ~ Health Issues ~ Weight Loss
- Pineal Gland Activation ~ Re-connection to Creator
- Cellular Toning ~ Sound & Color Emotional Healing
- DNA Activation ~ Release ~ Re-patterning
- Healing Shadow/Dark Night Experiences
- Sub-Personality ~ Entity Release
- Michelle is the developer and facilitator of the Christ Ray healing technique that she has taught worldwide.

**Included in all of Michelle's private healing sessions and workshops is the re-connection to your higher self, Mother-Father-Creator and your inner children.**

Michelle is currently living in Sedona, Arizona. She is available to provide her experiential evenings, lectures, workshops, and private sessions worldwide. Michelle also offers long-distance phone sessions. Because her work transcends time and distance, a phone session has the same powerful experience and healing as if you had been with her in-person.

By participating in Michelle's workshops and private sessions, the areas of your life that hold you back, that create concern and conflict, will easily shift and change. You will experience great healing and changes in your mental, emotional, and physical bodies. You will shift unwanted aspects of your personality and release fears, phobias, low self-esteem, past difficult patterns and experiences, trauma, feelings of being unloved, loneliness, and many other imbalanced areas of your life.

For more information about Michelle, her work, or to request evenings, lectures, workshops, or phone sessions, go to:

**www.SoulsAwakening.com**
**www.CreatorSpeaks.com**

CPSIA information can be obtained at www.ICGtesting.com
Printed in the USA
LVOW100837191112

307413LV00004B/5/P